Complete Study Edition

Carrie Hudspeth

W9-BDN-431

The Tempest

Commentary | Complete Text | Glossary

edited by
SIDNEY LAMB

Associate Professor of English,
Sir George Williams University, Montreal

Cliff's Notes
INCORPORATED

LINCOLN, NEBRASKA   68501

SBN   8220-1440-8

Copyright © 1966, 1965

by

C. K. Hillegass

All Rights Reserved

Printed in U.S.A.

Originally published under the title
"The Tempest: Complete Study Guide,"
copyright © 1965.

The Tempest

SHAKESPEARE WAS NEVER MORE MEANINGFUL—

. . . than when read in Cliff's "Complete Study Edition." The introductory sections give you all of the background information about the author and his work necessary for reading with understanding and appreciation. A descriptive bibliography provides guidance in the selection of works for further study. The inviting three-column arrangement of the complete text offers the maximum in convenience to the reader. Adjacent to the text there is a running commentary that provides clear supplementary discussion of the play as it develops. Obscure words and obsolete usages used by Shakespeare are explained in the glosses directly opposite to the line in which they occur. The numerous allusions are also clarified.

SIDNEY LAMB—

. . . the editor of this Shakespeare "Complete Study Edition," attended Andover Academy and Columbia University, receiving the Prince of Wales Medal for Philosophy and the Moyes Travelling Fellowship. Following graduate studies in Elizabethan literature at King's College, Cambridge, from 1949 to 1952, he became a member of the English Faculty of the University of London's University of the Gold Coast in West Africa. Professor Lamb joined the faculty of Sir George Williams University, Montreal, in 1956.

The Tempest
Contents

th bene fundry times publiquely
ht Honoyrable the Lord Cham
his Seruants.

THE MOST EX-
cellent and lamentable
Tragedie, of Romeo
and *Iuliet*.

an introduction

THE
Tragicall Historie of
HAMLET,
Prince of Denmarke.

By William Shakefpeare.

Newly imprinted and enlarged to almoſt as much againe as it was, according to the true and perfect Coppie.

AT LONDON,
Printed by I. R. for N. L. and are to be fold at his ſhoppe vnder Saint Dunſtons Church in

Two books are essential to the library of any English-speaking household; one of these is the Bible and the other is the works of William Shakespeare. These books form part of the house furnishings, not as reading material generally, but as the symbols of religion and culture—sort of a twentieth-century counterpart of the ancient Roman household gods. This symbolic status has done a great deal of damage both to religion and to Shakespeare.

Whatever Shakespeare may have been, he was not a deity. He was a writer of popular plays, who made a good living, bought a farm in the country, and retired at the age of about forty-five to enjoy his profits as a gentleman. The difference between Shakespeare and the other popular playwrights of his time was that he wrote better plays—plays that had such strong artistic value that they have been popular ever since. Indeed, even today, if Shakespeare could col-

William to Shakespeare

lect his royalties, he would be among the most prosperous of playwrights.

During the eighteenth century but mostly in the nineteenth, Shakespeare's works became "immortal classics," and the cult of Shakespeare-worship was inaugurated. The plays were largely removed from their proper place on the stage into the library where they became works of literature rather than drama and were regarded as long poems, attracting all the artistic and psuedo-artistic atmosphere surrounding poetry. In the nineteenth century this attitude was friendly but later, and especially in the early twentieth century, a strange feeling arose in the English-speaking world that poetry was sissy stuff, not for men but for "pansies" and women's clubs. This of course is sheer nonsense.

This outline will present a detailed analysis of the play and background information which will show the play in its proper perspective. This means seeing the play in relation to the other plays, to the history of the times when they were written, and in relation to the theatrical technique required for their successful performance.

G. B. Harrison's book *Introducing Shakespeare*, published by Penguin Books, will be of value for general information about Shakespeare and his plays. For reference material on the Elizabethan Theater, consult E. K. Chambers, *The Elizabethan Theatre* (four volumes). For study of the organization and production methods of this theater see *Henslowe's Diary* edited by W. W. Greg. Again for general reading the student will enjoy Margaret Webster's *Shakespeare Without Tears,* published by Whittlesey House (McGraw-Hill) in 1942.

The remainder of the Introduction will be divided into sections discussing Shakespeare's life, his plays, and his theater.

LIFE OF WILLIAM SHAKESPEARE

From the standpoint of one whose main interest lies with the plays themselves, knowledge of Shakespeare's life is not very important. Inasmuch as it treats of the period between 1592 and 1611, when the plays were being written, knowledge of his life is useful in that it may give some clues as to the topical matters introduced into the plays. For instance, the scene of Hamlet's advice to the players (Act III Scene ii) takes on an added significance when considered along with the fame and bombastic style of Edward Alleyn, the then famous actor-manager of the Lord Admiral's Players (the most powerful rivals of Shakespeare's company).

This biography is pieced together from the surviving public records of the day, from contemporary references in print, and from the London Stationer's Register. It is by no means complete. The skeletal nature of the biographical material available to scholars has led commentators in the past to invent part of the story to fill it out. These parts have frequently been invented by men who were more interested in upholding a private theory than in telling the truth, and this habit of romancing has led to a tradition of inaccurate Shakespearian biography. For this reason this outline may be of use in disposing of bad traditions.

In the heyday of the self-made man, the story developed that Shakespeare was a poor boy from the village, virtually uneducated, who fled from Stratford to London to escape prosecution for poaching on the lands of Sir Thomas Lucy, and there by his talent and a commendable industry raised himself to greatness. This rags-to-riches romance was in the best Horatio Alger tradition but was emphatically not true. The town records of Stratford make it clear that John Shakespeare, father of the playwright, was far from a pauper. He was a wealthy and responsible citizen who held in turn several municipal offices. He married (1557) Mary Arden, the daughter of a distinguished Catholic family. William, their third son, was baptized in the Parish Church in 1564. He had a good grammar school education. Ben Jonson's remark that Shakespeare had "small Latin and less Greek" did not mean the same in those days, when the educated man had a fluent command of

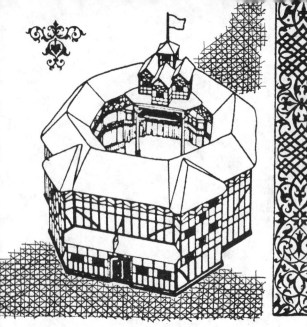

Exterior view of "The Globe"

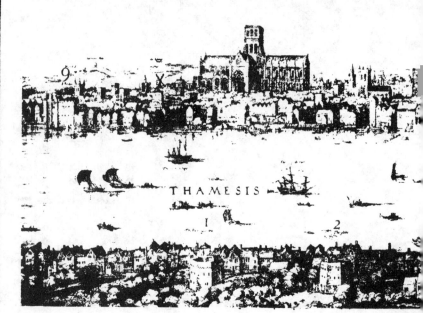

Shakespeare's London

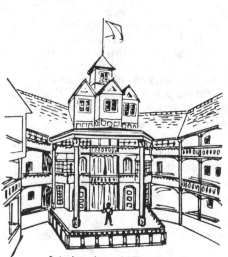

Interior view of "The Globe"

an introduction to Shakespeare

Latin and probably at least a reading knowledge of Greek, as it does now when classical scholars are few. The remark has been construed by the Horatio Alger people as meaning that Shakespeare reached London a semiliterate bumpkin; it is nonsense. It means merely that Shakespeare was not a university man, as most of the writers were, and that the University Wits were taking out their jealousy in snobbery and pointing out that Shakespeare used less purely literary symbolism than they did.

Shakespeare married Ann Hathaway when he was eighteen years old. She was some years older than he and the marriage seems to have been a rather hasty affair. Five months after the marriage, Suzanna, the first child, was born. Two years later, in 1585, twins Hamnet and Judith were baptized.

No one knows when Shakespeare came to London. The first mention of him occurs in the bad-tempered pamphlet which Robert Greene, one of the University Wits and a famous playwright, wrote just before his death. Greene complains of "an upstart crow, beautified with our feathers, that with his tiger's heart wrapped in a player's hide, supposes he is as well able to bombast out a blank verse as the best of you; and being an absolute Yohannes factotum, is in his own conceit the only Shakescene in a country." This was written in 1592 and indicates not only that Shakespeare was in London at the time, but that he was writing plays and beginning to make such a name for himself as to call forth the jealous apprehension of an established writer.

The next year, 1593, was a year of plague, and by order of the Lord Mayor and the Aldermen, the theaters were closed. The players, disorganized by this action, went on tour outside of London. During this year Shakespeare's two long poems, *Venus and Adonis* and *The Rape of Lucrece,* were entered in the Stationer's Register. Both were dedicated to the Earl of Southampton.

The public theaters had not been established very long. The first of these, called the Theatre, was built for James Burbage in 1576. By 1594, there were three such theaters in London, the two new houses being the Curtain and the Rose. By 1594, also, the three most celebrated of the writers, Kyd, Greene, and Marlowe were dead, and Shakespeare had already a considerable reputation. Before this date the theaters had been largely low class entertainment and the plays had been of rather poor quality. Through the revival of classical drama in the schools (comedies) and the Inns of Court (tragedies), an interest had been created in the stage. The noblemen of the time were beginning to attend the public theaters, and their tastes demanded a better class of play.

Against the background of this

increasing status and upper-class popularity of the theaters, Shakespeare's company was formed. After the 1594 productions under Alleyn, this group of actors divided. Alleyn formed a company called the Lord Admiral's Company which played in Henslowe's Rose Theatre. Under the leadership of the Burbages (James was the owner of the Theatre and his son Richard was a young tragic actor of great promise), Will Kemp (the famous comedian), and William Shakespeare, the Lord Chamberlain's company came into being. This company continued throughout Shakespeare's career. It was renamed in 1603, shortly after Queen Elizabeth's death, becoming the King's players.

The company played at the Theatre until Burbage's lease on the land ran out. The landlord was not willing to come to satisfactory terms. The company moved across the river and built the new Globe theater. The principal sharers in the new place were Richard and Cuthbert Burbage each with two and a half shares and William Shakespeare, John Heminge, Angustus Phillips, Thomas Pope, and Will Kemp, each with one share.

Burbage had wanted to establish a private theater and had rented the refectory of the old Blackfriars' monastery. Not being allowed to use this building he leased it to a man called Evans who obtained permission to produce plays acted by chil-dren. This venture was so successful as to make keen competition for the existing companies. This vogue of child actors is referred to in *Hamlet*, Act II Scene ii.

The children continued to play at Blackfriars until, in 1608, their license was suspended because of the seditious nature of one of their productions. By this time the public attitude towards the theaters had changed, and Burbage's Company, now the King's players, could move into the Blackfriars theater.

Partners with the Burbages in this enterprise were Shakespeare, Heminge, Condell, Sly, and Evans. This was an indoor theater, whereas the Globe had been outdoors. The stage conditions were thus radically altered. More scenery could be used; lighting effects were possible. Shakespeare's works written for this theater show the influence of change in conditions.

To return to the family affairs of the Shakespeares, records show that in 1596 John Shakespeare was granted a coat of arms and, along with his son, was entitled to call himself "gentleman." In this year also, William Shakespeare's son Hamnet died. In 1597 William Shakespeare bought from William Underwood a sizable estate at Stratford, called New Place.

Shakespeare's father died in 1601, his mother, in 1608. Both of his daughters married, one in 1607, the other in 1616.

During this time, Shakespeare went on acquiring property in Stratford. He retired to New Place probably around 1610 although this date is not definitely established, and his career as a dramatist was practically at an end. *The Tempest*, his last complete play, was written around the year 1611.

The famous will, in which he left his second best bed to his wife, was executed in 1616 and later on in that same year he was buried.

THE PLAYS

Thirty-seven plays are customarily included in the works of William Shakespeare. Scholars have been at great pains to establish the order in which these plays were written. The most important sources of information for this study are the various records of performances which exist, the printed editions which came out during Shakespeare's career, and such unmistakable references to current events as may crop up in the plays. The effect of the information gathered in this way is generally to establish two dates between which a given play must have been written. In *Hamlet* for instance, there is a scene in which Hamlet refers to the severe competition given to the adult actors by the vogue for children's performances. This vogue first became a serious threat to the professional companies in about 1600. In 1603 a very bad edition was published, without authorization, of *The*

Elizabethan types

Lute, standing cup, stoop

Queen Elizabeth

an introduction to Shakespeare

Tragical History of Hamlet, Prince of Denmark by William Shakespeare. These two facts indicate that *Hamlet* was written between the years of 1600 and 1603. This process fixed the order in which most of the plays were written. Those others of which no satisfactory record could be found were inserted in their logical place in the series according to the noticeable development of Shakespeare's style. In these various ways we have arrived at the following chronological listing of the plays.

1591 *Henry VI Part I*
      Henry VI Part II
      Henry VI Part III
      Richard III
      Titus Andronicus
      Love's Labour Lost
      The Two Gentlemen of Verona
      The Comedy of Errors
      The Taming of the Shrew

1594 *Romeo and Juliet*
      A Midsummer Night's Dream
      Richard II
      King John
      The Merchant of Venice

1597 *Henry IV Part I*
      Henry IV Part II
      Much Ado About Nothing
      Merry Wives of Windsor
      As You Like It
      Julius Caesar
      Henry V
      Troilus and Cressida

1601 *Hamlet*
      Twelfth Night
      Measure for Measure
      All's Well That Ends Well

      Othello
1606 *King Lear*
      Macbeth
      Timon of Athens
      Antony and Cleopatra
      Coriolanus
1609 *Pericles*
1611 *Cymbeline*
      The Winter's Tale
      The Tempest
      Henry VIII

At this point it is pertinent to review the tradition of dramatic form that had been established before Shakespeare began writing. Drama in England sprang at the outset from the miracle and morality plays of the medieval guilds. These dramatized Bible stories became increasingly less religious as time passed until finally they fell into disrepute. The next development was the writing of so-called *interludes*. These varied in character but often took the form of bawdy farce. As the renaissance gathered force in England, Roman drama began to be revived at the schools and the Inns of Court. Before long English writers were borrowing plots and conventions wholesale from the classic drama. The Italian model was the most fashionable and consequently was largely adopted, but many features of the old *interludes* still persisted, especially in plays written for the public theaters.

With the development among the nobility of a taste for the theater, a higher quality of work became in demand. Very few of

10

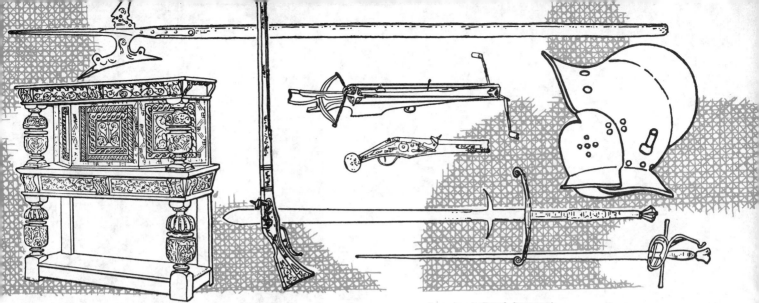

Court cupboard, crossbow, guns, sword, rapier, halberd, burgonet ·

the very early plays have survived. The reason for this is that the plays were not printed to be read; no one considered them worth the trouble. A play was strung together out of a set of stock characters and situations with frantic haste, often by as many as a dozen different men. These men who worked on plays did not regard their writing activity as of prime importance. They were primarily actors. With the cultivation of taste for better plays came the idea that the work of a playwright was an effort demanding special skill. The highborn audiences were interested in the plays themselves and began to include editions of their favorite plays in their libraries. With this demand for printed copies of the plays, the conception began of the dramatist as an artist in his own right, whether or not he acted himself (as most of them did).

By 1592, when Shakespeare began to make his personal reputation, a set of traditions had developed. This body of traditions gave Shakespeare the basic materials with which to work.

A special type of comedy writing had developed, centered around the name of John Lyly, designed for the sophisticated audience of the court and presented with lavish dances and decorative effects. This type of play was characterized by a delicately patterned artificiality of speech. The dialogue was studded with complicated references to Latin and Italian literature that the renaissance had made fashionable.

Shakespeare used this method extensively. In the early plays (before *The Merchant of Venice*) he was experimenting and wrote much that is nothing more than conventional. Later on, as his mature style developed, the writing becomes integral with and indispensable to the play and no longer appears artificial. In *Romeo and Juliet,* an early play, the following lines are spoken by Lady Capulet in urging Juliet to accept the Count Paris for her husband. These lines are brilliant but artificial, and the play seems to pause in order that this trick bit of word-acrobatics may be spoken.

Read o'er the volume of young
    Paris' face,
And find delight, writ there
    with beauty's pen.
Examine every married linea-
    ment,
And see how one another lends
    content:
And what obscured in this fair
    volume lies,
Find written in the margent of
    his eyes.
This precious book of love, this
    unbound lover,
To beautify him only needs a
    cover!

The other most important dramatic tradition was that of tragedy. The Elizabethan audiences liked spectacular scenes; they also had a great relish for scenes of sheer horror. This led to a school of tragic writing made popular by Kyd and Marlowe.

These plays were full of action and color and incredible wickedness, and the stage literally ran with artificial blood. Shakespeare's early tragedies are directly in this tradition, but later the convention becomes altered and improved in practice, just as that of comedy had done. The scene in *King Lear* where Gloucester has his eyes torn out stems from this convention. Lear, however, is a comparatively late play and the introduction of this scene does not distort or interrupt its organization.

Shakespeare's stylistic development falls into a quite well-defined progression. At first he wrote plays according to the habit of his rivals. He very quickly began experimenting with his technique. His main concern seems to be with tricks of language. He was finding out just what he could do. These early plays use a great deal of rhyme, seemingly just because Shakespeare liked writing rhyme. Later on, rhyme is used only when there is a quite definite dramatic purpose to justify it. Between the early plays and those which may be called mature (*The Merchant of Venice* is the first of the mature plays), there is a basic change in method. In the early works Shakespeare was taking his patterns from previous plays and writing his own pieces, quite consciously incorporating one device here and another there.

In the later period these tricks of the trade had been tested and

The world as known in 1600

Elizabethan coins

absorbed; they had become not contrived methods but part of Shakespeare's mind. This meant that, quite unconsciously, while his total attention was focused on the emotional and intellectual business of writing a masterpiece, he wrote in terms of the traditional habits he had learned and used in the earlier period. (*Henry IV, Julius Caesar, Henry V*, and *Hamlet* are the plays of this advanced stage.)

The group of plays between 1606 and 1609 shows a further new development. Having reached mastery of his medium in terms of dramatic technique (with *Othello*) and of power over the tension of thought in moving easily through scenes of comedy, pathos, and tragedy, he turned again to the actual literary quality of his plays and began to enlarge his scope quite beyond and apart from the theatrical traditions of his day. The early results of this new attempt are the two plays *King Lear* and *Macbeth*. The change in these plays is in the direction of concentration of thought. The attempt is, by using masses of images piled one on another, to convey shadings and intensities of emotion not before possible. He was trying to express the inexpressible. For example the following is from the last part of

an introduction
to Shakespeare

Lady Macbeth's famous speech in Act I, Scene v:

> Come, thick night,
> And pall thee in the dunnest smoke of hell,
> That my keen knife see not the wound it makes,
> Nor heaven peep through the blanket of the dark,
> To cry, hold, hold!

Compare the concentrated imagery of this speech with Hamlet's soliloquy at the end of Act III, Scene ii.

> 'Tis now the very witching time of night,
> When churchyards yawn, and hell itself breathes out
> Contagion to this world: now could I drink hot blood,
> And do such bitterness as the day
> Would quake to look on.

The sentiment of these two speeches is similar, but the difference in method is striking and produces a difference again in the type of effect. The *Lear-Macbeth* type of writing produces a higher tension of subtlety but tends to collect in masses rather than to move in lines as the lighter, more transparent writing of *Hamlet* does.

Shakespeare's last plays were conceived for the new indoor theater at Blackfriars and show this is in a more sophisticated type of staging. In *The Tempest*, last and most celebrated of these late comedies, there is dancing, and much complicated staging (such as the disappearing banquet, the ship at sea, and so on). The writing of plays for the

more distinguished audience of Blackfriars, and the increased stage resources there provided, influenced the form of the plays.

The writing of these plays forms a culmination. In his early apprenticeship Shakespeare had been extravagant in word-acrobatics, testing the limits of his technique. In the Lear-Macbeth period of innovation he had tried the limits of concentrated emotion to the point almost of weakening the dramatic effectiveness of the plays. In *The Tempest* his lines are shaken out into motion again. He seems to have been able to achieve the subtlety he was after in verse of light texture and easy movement, no longer showing the tendency to heaviness or opacity visible in *King Lear* and *Macbeth*.

THE THEATER

The first public theater in London was built in the year 1576 for James Burbage and was called simply The Theatre. Before this time players' companies had performed for the public in the courtyards of the city inns. For a more select public they frequently played in the great halls of institutions, notably the Inns of Court. The stage and auditorium of the Elizabethan theater were based on these traditions and combined features of both the hall and the inn-yard. The auditorium was small. There was a pit where the orchestra seats would be in a modern playhouse; this section was for the lowest classes who stood during the performances. Around the

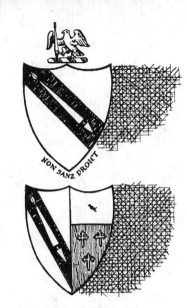

Shakespeare's Coat of Arms

Wood cut camp illustration

wall was a gallery for the gentry. The galleries and the tiring-house behind the fore-stage were roofed; the rest was open to the sky. The stage consisted of a very large platform that jutted out so that the pit audience stood on three sides of it. Behind this, under the continuation behind the stage of the gallery, was the inner stage; this was supplied with a curtain, but the open fore-stage was not. Above this inner stage was a balcony (really a continuation of the gallery), forming still another curtained stage. This gallery was used for kings addressing subjects from balconies, for the storming of walls, for Juliet's balcony and bedroom, for Cleopatra's monument and so on. Costumes and properties were extravagant (such as guillotines, fountains, ladders, etc.); extensive music was constantly used and such sound effects as cannon, drums, or unearthly screams were common; but there was no painted scenery as we know it; there was no darkness to focus attention on the stage, no facilities for stage-lighting. All these things are in marked contrast to the modern stage conventions and thus a serious problem of adaptation is posed when it comes to producing the plays under present day conditions.

The advantages are not all with the modern stage. It is true that the modern or picture stage can do more in the way of realistic effects, but this kind of realism is not important to good

drama. In fact there has been a recent trend away from realistic scenery in the theater back to a conventional or stylized simplicity.

One effect of Shakespeare's stage upon his work was to make the scenes in the plays more person-scenes than place-scenes. As a matter of fact in many cases the places assigned in the texts to various scenes were not in the original and have only been added by an editor who did not understand this very fact.

It used to be said that *Antony and Cleopatra* could not be staged and was written to be read rather than acted. The grounds for this statement were that in the fourth act there were no less than fourteen scenes. To some, a scene means a change of place and requires a break in the play while scenery is shifted. To Shakespeare these scenes meant no such thing; they meant, simply, that there were fourteen different groupings of people, successively and without any break, carrying on the action of the play. The scene headings when added should have been (1) Caesar, (2) Antony and Cleopatra, (3) the common soldiers, etc., instead of (1) Before Alexandria, (2) Alexandria, a room in the palace, etc. By this you may see that with all its limitations, the Elizabethan stage had a measure of flexibility that the modern stage could envy.

Fashions in staging Shakespeare have altered radically in the last few years. At the close

of the nineteenth century, Sir Herbert Beerbohm Tree staged a spectacular series of pageant productions. All the tricks of romantic realistic staging were used and, if necessary, the play was twisted, battered, and re-written to accommodate the paraphernalia.

The modern method is to produce the plays as nearly according to the text as possible and work out a compromise to achieve the sense of space and of flexibility necessary, yet without departing so far from the stage habits of today as to confuse or divert the audience. This technique was inaugurated by Granville-Barker in the early twentieth century. With the exception of such extravagant stunts as Orson Welles' production of *Julius Caesar* in modern dress (set in Chicago and complete with tommy-guns), the prevailing practice now is to use simple, stylized scenery adapted to the needs of producing the play at full length.

Much can be done in the way of learning Shakespeare through books, but the only sure way is to see a well produced performance by a good company of actors. Whatever genius Shakespeare may have possessed as a psychologist, philosopher, or poet, he was first of all a man of the theater, who knew it from the inside, and who wrote plays so well-plotted for performance that from his day up to the present, no great actor has been able to resist them.

MIRANDA and FERDINAND, Lovers

an introduc

SHAKESPEARE'S LAST PLAYS

The Tempest is one of a group of plays (the others being *Pericles, Cymbeline,* and *The Winter's Tale*) written at the end of Shakespeare's career as a playwright, and often referred to as the romances or the tragicomedies. Although neither of these terms is really satisfactory, they both indicate qualities that all these plays have in common. Like the medieval and Renaissance romances, their stories are really farfetched fantasies, with love as a central concern. They show a complete disregard for the laws of everyday causality: Prospero's magic—the vanishing banquets and invisible music—are typical. In this they satisfied the theatrical taste of the early seventeenth century for improbable romantic fantasies. We must always remember that while the events and situations in a romance are often improbable, the characters' emotions and attitudes are real enough. The plays are tragicomic in that, while they end happily (the original definition of "comic"), they include tragic elements that suggest the possibility of an other-than-happy ending. This tragic element usually takes the form of some evil or malevolent character whose machinations are revealed, then overcome in the course of the play. In *The Tempest* Caliban's attempted assault on Miranda, his plot to "paunch" Prospero with a stake or "cut his wesand with a knife;" and the Antonio-Sebastian plot against the lives of Alonso and Gonzalo are such potentially tragic elements. In *The Tempest,* as in the other romances, while we know that the ultimate outcome is a happy one, we are constantly reminded that the world contains evil, and that Prospero's victory is only won by constant vigilance, and an understanding of the malignity of which humanity is capable.

As with the other romances, the surface action of *The Tempest* is simple enough. At the lowest level it can be seen as a kind of fairy tale, complete with good and bad characters, a pure, uncomplicated love, and a good deal of miraculous incident — magic storms, charms that paralyze the evil characters and protect the good, and even a play-within-the-play featuring mythological deities. It is exciting

14

PROSPERO, Exiled Duke of Milan

tion to The Tempest

theater of the kind that Shakespeare consistently provides. Yet, like the other romances, it is much more than this. In his final works Shakespeare seems to have summed up and compressed several of the themes that he had experimented with in his earlier drama. Some of these themes are outlined below as they appear in *The Tempest*; in each case there is a more elaborate treatment in the commentary which accompanies the individual scenes.

THEMES OF "THE TEMPEST"

For all the simplicity of its action, the play is rich in meanings, making interpretation both inviting and difficult. As Mark Van Doren has written: "*The Tempest* binds up in final form a host of themes with which its author has been concerned. . . . The play seems to order itself in terms of its meanings; things in it stand for other things, so that we are tempted to search its 'dark backward' for a single meaning, quite final for Shakespeare and quite abstract. The trouble is that the meanings are not self-evident. One interpreta-

tion of *The Tempest* does not agree with another. And there is a deeper trouble in the truth that any interpretation, even the wildest, is more or less plausible. . . . Any set of symbols, moved close to the play, lights up as in an electric field." We must always recall that no play by Shakespeare, and indeed no great play, can be reduced to a prosaic explanatory meaning. A great play is a representation and perhaps an interpretation of life, but not an explanation of it. There are, however, several coherent strands of meaning woven into the action of *The Tempest*. They are, to oversimplify somewhat, the ideas of atonement and reconciliation, of purification through suffering, and of the contrast between nature and society.

The story of *The Tempest*, which begins before the play opens, tells us that Prospero, the Duke of Milan, allowed his dukedom to be usurped by his brother Antonio, with the connivance of Alonso, King of Naples. This is the evil act that begins the chain of events which ends in the play itself. In the course of the play Alonso suffers the loss of his son

Ferdinand and in his grief (and under Ariel's direction) he recalls his sin against Prospero, repents of it, and is, in the end, reconciled with Prospero. He has atoned for the evil he has done. The reconciliation is cemented by the marriage of Ferdinand to Prospero's daughter Miranda. Sin, atonement and reconciliation is a common pattern in Shakespeare's last plays. It is usually given expression in the love of the members of a younger generation, who in their innocence somehow cancel the strife and betrayal of their elders. Thus the happy ending of Shakespeare's romances, and *The Tempest*, is far more than a plot device making everything come out all right in the end. It is a dramatic statement of the way in which the evil that men do to one another can be overcome by good, and affirmation that the innocence and good faith of youth is more powerful than the ambition and malevolence of age.

The second, or purification, theme is more elaborate. The ship's passengers who are wrecked on Prospero's island are divided at the play's beginning

STEPHANO, the Butler — CALIBAN, the Slave — TRINCULO, the Jester

into several groups; each goes through a purgatorial trial of some kind. In each case the reactions are different. Alonso and the court party set off in search of Ferdinand, whom they believe drowned. They are confronted by an illusory banquet (symbolizing the pleasures of sense and greed) which vanishes when they approach it. They—Alonso, Sebastian, and Antonio — are then denounced as "men of sin" by Ariel and are driven into a frenzy of madness. It is significant that Gonzalo, the "honest old councilor" and a man of innocence and good will, is unaffected either by the vision of the banquet or the denunciation; he needs no trial or suffering. Alonso is deeply affected; believing the death of his son to be a punishment, he confesses his guilt and seeks to atone for it. He is purified through the trial, and reconciled with Prospero at the play's end. Neither Antonio nor Sebastian, who are equally

an introduction to the Tempest

guilty, are affected in this way. They remain impenitent. Their incapacity for remorse is punished, Ariel suggests, by a "ling'ring perdition (worse than any death/ Can be at once)."

Ferdinand is left to wander by himself on the island. He is innocent of any evil and is guided by Ariel to Miranda, with whom he immediately falls in love. He must undergo his trial and suffering which takes the form of woodbearing servitude to Prospero. However, Ferdinand recognizes the nature of his trial. He realizes that only through servitude and suffering can he win his freedom and the object of his desire—Miranda for his wife.

Stephano, the drunken butler, and Trinculo, the clown, form a third group. They blunder about the island in a haze of confusion and inebriation and, under the guidance of Caliban, plot to overthrow Prospero. Their trial and suffering takes two forms. First they are submerged in a horse pond, then harried and hunted by Prospero's dogs. They are comic characters and their trials are comic. They learn nothing from what happens to them. The plays leaves them as it found them. They are not admirable, but neither do they represent the sort of evil we see in Antonio and Sebastian.

Thus the various elements of the shipwrecked group (who represent society in a compressed form) react variously to the experience of the island. Alonso has the capacity to understand himself and benefits; so does Ferdinand, in whose case love confers understanding. Antonio and Sebastian cannot learn, and remain corrupt; Stephano and Trinculo are beneath any kind of moral enlightenment.

One of the most pervasive themes of *The Tempest* is the contrast between nature and society. Caliban is the central figure here. Caliban's name is probably an anagram of "cannibal." In creating him, Shakespeare may well have had in mind an essay by the French philosopher Montaigne. This essay, "Of Cannibals," certainly lies behind that passage in the play in which Gonzalo outlines his ideal commonwealth (see commentary at II,i. 150-158). In the essay Montaigne questions the conventional Renaissance view that society is by definition good, that man outside of society, in his natural state, is by definition bad. This view was fundamentally a religious one. For the orthodox Renaissance thinker, society with its rules, obligations, and hierarchical order was a divine creation. It is this notion of a divine order in society that

The Enchanted Isle

CALIBAN, Prospero's savage Slave

lies behind Shakespeare's historical plays and also behind the historical doctrine of the divine right of kings. Since society was a divinely created organism, those beings who existed outside of organized society, were regarded as being little better than the beasts. This seems a strange view to us, but it was commonly held and accounts, for example, for much of the inhumanity shown to the natives of Africa and the New World by the Elizabethan explorers. Existing beyond society or civilization these natives were not, in one sense, fully human. Against this belief Montaigne argued that men, like plants, flourish as well or better in a natural, ungoverned state as in the artificial organization of society (see the quote from Montaigne's essay in the commentary). Gonzalo puts Montaigne's view in his disquisition at II.i., arguing for a "commonwealth" in which there should be no "name of magistrate" (i.e., legal rule), no "riches, poverty" (i.e., private ownership) and men would thrive in a state of natural freedom. This notion of the superiority of the natural condition of man over his artificial, social, condition gained ground in the seventeenth and eighteenth centuries. It lies behind Rousseau's *Social Contract* and the social

theories of the Romantics of the nineteenth century. It also gave rise to the complementary theory of the "noble savage," which held that man in a state of nature was a purer and more innocent being than social man. This aspect of the theory is exemplified in the figure of Caliban.

Gonzalo's version of Montaigne's natural state is a piece of well meant idealism but, as the remarks of Sebastian and Antonio show, it is also somewhat unrealistic. Caliban is the real answer to Gonzalo's glorification of the natural, the noble savage. However, Caliban is "a thing most brutish" on whose "nature," as Prospero says, "nurture will never stick." Here Prospero represents control, reason, and discipline. By "nurture" he means training, education, spiritual development, and indeed all that we mean by civilization. Caliban is the animal instinct that resents and rejects "nurture," and the opposition of the two figures through the play is the opposition between civilization and nature. As so often in Shakespeare, a further qualification is necessary. Caliban may represent degenerate animal nature, but he is not entirely evil. It is significant that he is given some of the most lyrical poetry in the play. There is a sense in which his intuitive understand-

ing of the natural world has a sensitivity which the "civilized" visitors to the island lack (see commentary at I.ii and III.ii). Caliban may be a "deboshed fish," and a "monster," but he is not evil in the calculating, cold-blooded way Antonio is. While civilization is a positive value in the play, it can produce distortions and perversions (as in Antonio and Sebastian) that are far worse than anything in Caliban's "natural" bestiality.

DATE, SOURCES, AND TEXT

There is external evidence to show that *The Tempest* was first performed in 1611 in a notation from the "Revels Account" (the Revels Office supervised all dramatic performances for the Court of King James): "By the King's players: Hallowmass night [November 1] was presented at Whitehall before the King's Majesty a play called The Tempest." The play was revived and presented again in the winter of 1612-13, along with fourteen others, as part of the elaborate entertainment offered to the Elector of Palatine, who had come to England to court and marry James's daughter, the Princess Elizabeth.

In contrast to his usual practice, Shakespeare does not seem to have borrowed the story of

17

ARIEL, the Spirit

FERDINAND and MIRANDA PLAY CHESS

The Tempest from any historical or fictional source. As the editors of the *New Cambridge* editions say, "those who must always be searching for a 'source' of every plot of Shakespeare's (as though he could invent nothing!) will be disappointed in *The Tempest*. . . . And, after all, what fairy tale or folk tale is commoner, the world over, than that which combines a witch or wizard, an only daughter, an adventurous prince caught and bound to carry logs, etc., with pity and confederate love to counteract the spell and bring all right in the end?" While it is true that there are no specific plot sources for the play, there are more general sources or influences in Montaigne's essay *"Of Cannibals"* (discussed above and in the commentary), and in a group of pamphlets published in 1610 and generally known as the "Bermuda pamphlets." These latter describe a wreck on the Bermudas in 1609; they caused a good deal

an introduction to the Tempest

of comment and excitement in England. Although Shakespeare's magic island is somewhere in the Mediterranean, there are a great many parallels between his play and the Bermuda pamphlets.

In May, 1609, a fleet of ships left England under Sir Thomas Gates and Sir George Summers for John Smith's new colony in Virginia. One of the ships, which carried both Gates and Summers, was separated from the rest by a storm and driven to the coast of the Bermudas where "she fell in between two rocks, where she was fast lodged and locked for further budging." Gates, Summers, and the crew got safely ashore with much of the ship's supplies; later they were able to reach Virginia. Meanwhile, they had been given up for lost in England, and their survival—reported in the pamphlets—seemed to have something of the miraculous about it. This disaster and its fortunate outcome may have excited Shakespeare's imagination. He knew the Bermuda pamphlets well, but seems to have relied particularly on William Strachey's *A True Repertory of the Wrack*. Here are some excerpts, with the point in the play to which they seem relevant.

I.i. The Storm.—". . . a dreadful storm and hideous began to

blow out of the Northeast, which swelling and roaring as it were by fits, at length did beat all light from heaven; which like a hell of darkness turned black upon us, so much the more full of horror, as in such cases horror and fear use to overrun the troubled, and overmastered senses of all, which (taken up with amazement) the ears lay so sensible to the terrible cries, and murmurs of the wind, and distraction of our company, as who was most armed and best prepared, was not a little shaken."

I.i. The Scene Aboard.—"Sometimes shrieks in our ship amongst women and passengers, not used to such hurly and discomforts, made us look one upon the other with troubled hearts, and panting bosoms: our clamours drowned in the winds, and the winds in thunder. Prayers might well be in the heart and lips, but drowned in the outcries of the officers: nothing heard that could give comfort, nothing seen that could encourage hope."

I.ii. Ariel: "I flamed amazement."—"Only upon the Thursday night, Sir George Summers being upon the watch, had an apparition of a little round light, like a faint star, trembling, and streaming along with a sparkling blaze, half the height upon the mainmast, and shooting sometimes from shroud to shroud,

18

ARIEL Obeys PROSPERO'S Command

tempting to settle as it were upon any of the four shrouds ... the Spaniards call it St. Elmo and have authentic and miraculous legends of it. ... Be it what it will, it could have served us now miraculously to have taken our height by it, it might have struck amazement, and a reverence in our devotions, according to the due of a miracle."

The Providential Quality of the Wreck. "Ferdinand: Though the seas threaten, they are merciful."—"We found it to be the dangerous and dreaded island, or rather islands, of the Bermudas ... they be called commonly the Devil's Islands, and are feared and avoided of all sea travellers alive above any place in the world. Yet it pleases our merciful God to make even this hideous and hated place both the place of our safety and means of our deliverance."

Plots and Conspiracies. — "In these dangerous and devilish disquiets (whilst the almighty God wrought for us and sent us, miraculously delivered from the calamities of the sea, all blessings upon the short to content and bind us to gratefulness) thus enraged amongst ourselves, to the destruction each of the other, into what mischief and misery had we been given up, had we not had a governor with his authority to have suppressed the

same? Yet was there a worse practice, faction, and conjuration afoot, deadly and bloody, in which the life of our governor with many others were threatened and could not but miscarry in his fall."

Most of Shakespeare's plays were printed both in Quarto editions during his lifetime, and in the collection made by two actors of his company, Heminge and Condell, in 1623 and called the *Folio* or First Folio. *The Tempest* was printed only in the *Folio,* and is a particularly "clean" text—that is, free from corruptions and inaccuracies in the copyreading and printing. Unlike the rest of the plays it has elaborate stage directions, presumably by Shakespeare, and regular, accurate punctuation. It is also divided into acts and scenes (which was unusual) and generally gives evidence of careful editing. This text follows the Folio with a very few minor departures and relineations.

Bibliography

EDITIONS

A New Variorum Edition of Shakespeare, ed. Horace H. Furness. New York: J. B. Lippincott, 1871——. (Reprints by The American Scholar and Dover Publications.) Each play is dealt with in a separate volume of monumental scholarship.

The Yale Shakespeare, ed. Helge Kökeritz and Charles T. Prouty. New Haven: Yale University Press, 1955——. A multi-volume edition founded on modern scholarship.

COMMENTARY AND CRITICISM

Bentley, G. E. *Shakespeare and His Theatre.* Lincoln: University of Nebraska Press, 1964 (paperback). Illuminating discussion of the actual conditions under which, and for which, Shakespeare wrote.

Bradley, A. C. *Shakespearean Tragedy: Lectures on Hamlet, Othello, King Lear, Macbeth.* New York: Macmillan, 1904. (Paperback ed.; New York: Meridian Books, 1955.) A classic examination of the great tragedies.

Chambers, Edmund K. *William Shakespeare: A Study of Facts and Problems,* 2 vols. Oxford: Clarendon Press, 1930. Indispensable source for bibliographical and historical information.

Chute, Marchette. *Shakespeare of London.* New York: E. P. Dutton, 1949. A vivid account of Shakespeare's career in the dynamic Elizabethan metropolis.

Granville-Barker, Harley. *Prefaces to Shakespeare.* London: Sidgwick & Jackson, 1927-47. (2 vols.; Princeton: Princeton University Press, 1947.) Stimulating studies of ten plays by a scholarly man of the theater.

Harbage, Alfred. *Shakespeare's Audience.* New York: Columbia University Press, 1941. Revealing approach to Shakespeare as a practical man of the theater.

Knight, Wilson. *The Wheel of Fire.* London: Oxford University Press, 1930. Stresses the power of intuition to capture the total poetic experience of Shakespeare's work.

Spurgeon, Caroline. *Shakespeare's Imagery and What It Tells Us.* Cambridge: Cambridge University Press, 1935. A psychological study of the playwright's imagery as a means to understanding the man himself.

20

The Tempest

Dramatis Personae

ALONSO, King of Naples.

SEBASTIAN, his brother.

PROSPERO, the right Duke of Milan.

ANTONIO, his brother, the usurping Duke of Milan.

FERDINAND, son to the King of Naples.

GONZALO, an honest old councilor.

ADRIAN and FRANCISCO, lords.

CALIBAN, a savage and deformed slave.

TRINCULO, a jester.

STEPHANO, a drunken butler.

Master of a ship.

Boatswain.

Mariners.

MIRANDA,
    daughter to Prospero.

ARIEL, an airy spirit.

IRIS

CERES   } presented

JUNO   } by

NYMPHS } spirits.

REAPERS

Other Spirits
attending
on Prospero.

SCENE-
A ship at sea:
an island

THE TEMPEST

ACT I SCENE I

The opening scene of a play always presents a problem to the playwright, and none solved it better than Shakespeare. So much is written concerning his genius, his penetrating understanding of character and the power of his poetry, that we sometimes forget that he was a skillful, practical man of the theater as well. He knew that the first scene must both grip the audience, and also impart to them something of the situation of the play. Many of Shakespeare's plays start in the middle of a tense debate—as that between the sentries in Hamlet, or the crowd in Coriolanus. In The Tempest the shouts between the Boatswain and Master, indicating the imminent destruction of their ship, will at once excite the interest and anticipation of the audience. Who are these characters? Will they, as they seem to think, perish in the storm? On the Elizabethan stage the balcony above the main stage was probably used as a part of the ship, where the Master appeared. The main stage was the ship's waist, where the Boatswain and the passengers argued with one another.

As well as providing a scene filled with violence and excitement, Shakespeare also begins to define his characters. This is done subtly, without direct explanation, but rather through the characters' varying attitudes toward the crisis. The Boatswain is all practical activity, issuing orders and urging his men. The social distinctions of rank are swept aside by the storm. He berates the court party (as they are usually called) who enter at 7 for their useless interruption. The court party (Alonso, Sebastian, Antonio, Ferdinand, Gonzalo, Adrian and Francisco) are also given some individual distinction. Shakespeare will elaborate on these distinctions later in the play. Sebastian and Antonio heap abuse on the sailors who are laboring to save them—"Hang, cur, hang, you whoreson, insolent noisemaker!" On the stage this probably ought to be played so as to suggest their fear. The crisis (as with the other crises in the play) reveals true character. It brings out the selfish viciousness of Sebastian and Antonio. Gonzalo, on the other hand —described in the Dramatis Personae as "an honest old councilor" —is every bit as frightened, but his reaction is to hope. He has even the courage for something like a jest. He considers that since the Boatswain, with his rough, uncivil talk looks as though he were "born to be hanged," the ship is sure to be saved. It is typical of the contrast between Antonio and Gonzalo that at the scene's end An-

---

ACT ONE, scene one.

(A Ship at Sea)

A tempestuous noise of thunder and lightning heard.
Enter a SHIPMASTER *and a* BOATSWAIN.

Master. Boatswain!

Boatswain. Here, master. What cheer?

Master. Good, speak to th' mariners; fall to't 3
yarely, or we run ourselves aground. Bestir, bestir! 4

Enter MARINERS.

Boatswain. Heigh, my hearts! Cheerly, cheerly, my hearts! Yare, yare! Take in the topsail! Tend to th' master's whistle! Blow till thou burst thy 7 wind, if room enough!

Enter ALONSO, SEBASTIAN, ANTONIO, FERDINAND, GONZALO *and* Others.

Alonso. Good boatswain, have care. Where's the master? Play the men. 10

Boatswain. I pray now, keep below.

Antonio. Where is the master, bos'n?

Boatswain. Do you not hear him? You mar our labor. Keep your cabins: you do assist the storm.

Gonzalo. Nay, good, be patient. 15

Boatswain. When the sea is. Hence! What cares 16 these roarers for the name of king? To cabin! Silence! Trouble us not!

Gonzalo. Good, yet remember whom thou hast aboard.

Boatswain. None that I more love than myself. You are a councilor: if you can command these elements to silence and work the peace of the present, we will not hand a rope more; use your au- 24 thority. If you cannot, give thanks you have lived so long, and make yourself ready in your cabin for the mischance of the hour, if it so hap.— Cheerily, good hearts!—Out of our way, I say. 28
[*Exit.*

Gonzalo. I have great comfort from this fellow: methinks he hath no drowning mark upon him; his complexion is perfect gallows. Stand fast, good Fate, 31 to his hanging! Make the rope of his destiny our cable, for our own doth little advantage. If he be not born to be hanged, our case is miserable.
[*Exeunt.*

Enter BOATSWAIN.

Boatswain. Down with the topmast! Yare! Lower, lower! Bring her to try with main-course! [*A cry* 36 *within.*] A plague upon this howling! They are louder than the weather or our office. 38

Enter SEBASTIAN, ANTONIO, *and* GONZALO.

Yet again? What do you here? Shall we give o'er 39 and drown? Have you a mind to sink?

Sebastian. A'pox o' your throat, you bawling, blas-

---

3. "Good": in answer to the boatswain's question.
4. "yarely": quickly, smartly.

7. "Blow . . .": addressed to the storm.

10. "Play": behave like.

15. "good": man, understood.
16. "What cares": a common Elizabethan use of the singular form of the verb with a plural subject.

24. "hand": i.e., handle.

28. "Cheerily, good hearts!": the boatswain addresses this to the sailors, and turns, with his next phrase, to brush the court party aside.

31. "complexion": his face, as an indication of character.
"Stand fast . . . hanging!": an allusion to the proverb 'Who's born to be hanged will never drown.'

36. "to try": to lie hull-to or hove-to.
"main-course": mainsail.

38. "louder than . . . office": i.e., the "howling" of the passengers makes more noise than either the weather or the sailors at their work ("office")

39. "Shall we give o'er": i.e., shall we give up, because of your interference, and drown?

23

THE TEMPEST

ACT I SCENE I

tonio can only speak in terms of abuse ("We are merely cheated of our lives by drunkards") and of revenge on those who seem unable to save him ("would thou might'st lie drowning"). Gonzalo, while he gives expression to his fear ("I would fain die a dry death"), suggests that all their lives are in the hands of some superhuman power ("The wills above be done"). This last wish in fact expresses the truth, although not in the way Gonzalo intends.

The opening storm gives the play its name and has some symbolic significance. It represents violence, and some kind of disruption. Storms usually have significance in Shakespeare—for example the storms which precede the assassination of Julius Caesar, and King Duncan, and the one which accompanies the suffering and insanity of King Lear. The action of The Tempest moves from this disharmony—which is in external nature and in some of the characters—toward a new harmony and peace. At the end of the play the sea is referred to again, when the characters prepare to return to Milan. The sea has then become serene and peaceful, the "calm seas, auspicious gales" that Prospero refers to at V.i.315. What seems at first to be destructive is, in the end, benign. As Ferdinand says at V.i.178: "Though the seas threaten, they are merciful./ I have cursed them without cause."

ACT I SCENE II

This scene, the longest in the play and one of the longest in all of Shakespeare's drama, may best be divided for comment into three parts: (1) Prospero's recapitulation of his and Miranda's story, (2) the introduction of Ariel and Caliban, and (3) Ariel's direction of Ferdinand to Prospero and Miranda

1. The scene opens with Miranda's vivid account of the shipwreck. We have already witnessed the fear and confusion aboard

---

phemous, incharitable dog!

Boatswain. Work you, then.

Antonio. Hang, cur, hang, you whoreson, insolent noisemaker! We are less afraid to be drowned than thou art.

Gonzalo. I'll warrant him for drowning, though the 47
ship were no stronger than a nutshell and as leaky
as an unstanched wench. 49

Boatswain. Lay her ahold, ahold! Set her two
courses! Off to sea again! Lay her off! 51

Enter MARINERS *wet.*

Mariners. All lost! To prayers, to prayers! All lost!
                                         [*Exeunt.*

Boatswain. What, must our mouths be cold?

Gonzalo. The King and Prince at prayers! Let's
  assist them,
For our case is as theirs.

Sebastian.   I am out of patience.

Antonio. We are merely cheated of our lives by
  drunkards. 56
This wide-chopped rascal — would thou mightst lie
  drowning 57
The washing of ten tides!

Gonzalo.   He'll be hanged yet, 58
Though every drop of water swear against it
And gape at wid'st to glut him. 60
[*A confused noise within:*] "Mercy on us! —
We split, we split! — Farewell, my wife and children! —
Farewell, brother! — We split, we split, we split!"
                            [*Exit* BOATSWAIN.

Antonio. Let's all sink with th' King.

Sebastian.   Let's take leave of him.
                        [*Exit with* ANTONIO.

Gonzalo. Now would I give a thousand furlongs of
sea for an acre of barren ground — long heath,
brown furze, anything. The wills above be done, but 67
I would fain die a dry death.   [*Exit.*

Scene two.

(BEFORE PROSPERO'S CELL)

Enter PROSPERO *and* MIRANDA.

Miranda. If by your art, my dearest father, you have 1
Put the wild waters in this roar, allay them.
The sky, it seems, would pour down stinking pitch
But that the sea, mounting to th' welkin's cheek, 4
Dashes the fire out. O, I have suffered
With those that I saw suffer! a brave vessel 6
(Who had no doubt some noble creature in her)
Dashed all to pieces! O, the cry did knock
Against my very heart! Poor souls, they perished!
Had I been any god of power, I would
Have sunk the sea within the earth or ere 11

---

47. "I'll warrant . . . drowning": I'll guarantee that he won't drown.

49. "unstanched": loose.

51. "Lay her ahold": i.e., a-hull, or hove-to. The boatswain immediately reverses this order ("Off to sea again!") when he sees there is no room to lie-to. The nautically minded Elizabethan audience would understand the crisis implied in this reversal. The sea-drenched mariners who now enter confirm the danger.

56. "merely": absolutely, completely.

57. "wide-chopped": wide-jawed—our loud-mouthed.

58. "The washing . . . tides": "An exaggerated form of the sentence passed upon pirates by the English court of Admiralty, which was that they should be hanged on the shore at low water mark and remain there until three tides had flowed and ebbed." (Arden edition)

60. "glut": to swallow.

67. "furze": gorse.

1. "art": here, the art of magic.

4. "welkin's cheek": face of the sky.

6. "brave": fine in appearance (as elsewhere in Shakespeare).

11. "or ere": before.

THE TEMPEST

the ship but the stage, especially the Elizabethan stage, cannot convey the visual sense of this kind of scene. What an audience watching a motion picture can be made to see, through the work of special effects technicians, the Elizabethan dramatist must describe. Shakespeare was aware of this limitation of the stage. He refers to it specifically in the opening chorus of Henry V, when the audience is asked to imagine what cannot be shown on the stage. Shakespeare there attempts "On this unworthy scaffold to bring forth/ So great an object: can this cockpit hold/ The vasty fields of France or may we cram/ Within this wooden O the very casques/ That did affright the air at Agincourt?" The audience is therefore asked to "Piece out our imperfections with your thoughts." It is noteworthy that Shakespeare through his dramatic poetry is able to tell the audience what it sees. His language, in effect, takes the place of our modern technical devices. It does more than this. It gives the visual effect and usually provides some emotional accompaniment or reaction to it. We have seen the storm from within the ship, in the cries of the Boatswain and the fear of the courtiers. Now Miranda's words suggest the whole scene, the "wild waters," the sky and the sea seeming to meet. She also communicates some of the terror of the scene, since she has "suffered with those that I saw suffer." This speech is given to Miranda for another reason: she is the person in the play who best exemplifies the virtues of innocence and love. These qualities are at once apparent in her immediate and unquestioning concern over the fate of the brave vessel which must carry, she thinks, "some noble creature."

Over a third of this long scene is taken with Prospero's account of the events that preceded the action of the play. Some such passage must occur in any play. The audience must be informed about the background of the situation they are watching. It is usually called the protasis or exposition. The exposition is par-

It should the good ship so have swallowed and
The fraughting souls within her.
    Prospero.   Be collected.   13
No more amazement. Tell your piteous heart   14
There's no harm done.
    Miranda.   O, woe the day!
    Prospero.   No harm.
I have done nothing but in care of thee,
Of thee my dear one, thee my daughter, who
Art ignorant of what thou art, naught knowing
Of whence I am; nor that I am more better   19
Than Prospero, master of a full poor cell,   20
And thy no greater father.
    Miranda.   More to know
Did never meddle with my thoughts.
    Prospero.   'Tis time   22
I should inform thee farther. Lend thy hand
And pluck my magic garment from me. So,
Lie there, my art. Wipe thou thine eyes; have
    comfort.   25
The direful spectacle of the wrack, which touched
The very virtue of compassion in thee,   27
I have with such provision in mine art   28
So safely ordered that there is no soul —
No, not so much perdition as an hair   30
Betid to any creature in the vessel   31
Which thou heard'st cry, which thou saw'st sink. Sit
    down;
For thou must now know farther.
    Miranda.   You have often
Begun to tell me what I am; but stopped
And left me to a bootless inquisition,   35
Concluding, "Stay: not yet."
    Prospero.   The hour's now come;
The very minute bids thee ope thine ear.
Obey, and be attentive. Canst thou remember
A time before we came unto this cell?
I do not think thou canst, for then thou wast not
Out three years old.
    Miranda.   Certainly, sir I can.   41
    Prospero. By what? By any other house or person?
Of any thing the image tell me that   43
Hath kept with thy remembrance.
    Miranda.   'Tis far off,
And rather like a dream than an assurance
That my remembrance warrants. Had I not   46
Four or five women once that tended me?
    Prospero. Thou hadst, and more, Miranda. But how
    is it
That this lives in thy mind? What seest thou else
In the dark backward and abysm of time?   50
If thou rememb'rest aught ere thou cam'st here,
How thou cam'st here thou mayst.
    Miranda.   But that I do not.
    Prospero. Twelve year since, Miranda, twelve year
    since,
Thy father was the Duke of Milan and
A prince of power.
    Miranda.   Sir, are not you my father?
    Prospero. Thy mother was a piece of virtue, and   56

13. "fraughting": forming the freight or cargo.
    "collected": calm, composed.
14. "amazement": consternation, as in Hamlet II.iv.112, "amazement on thy mother sits."
    "piteous": full of pity.

19. "more better": a double comparative, common in Elizabethan English.
20. "cell": used here in the Elizabethan sense of a small room, or dwelling, as in a monk's cell; on the Elizabethan stage Prospero's cell would be represented by the curtained inner stage.
22. "meddle": interfere, mingle.

25. "my art": i.e., his magic robe, which he here takes off, to resume it again at 169.
27. "the very virtue": the innermost essence.
28. "provision": prevision, foresight.
30. "perdition": loss.
31. "Betid": happened.

35. "bootless inquisition": profitless questioning.

41. "Out": fully.

43. "Of any . . . me": i.e., describe anything to me.

46. "remembrance warrants": that my memory can guarantee.

50. "backward and abysm": past and abyss.

56. "piece": perfect specimen

THE TEMPEST

ACT I SCENE II

ticularly lengthy in The Tempest because Shakespeare's way of constructing the play, differs from his usual method. As a rule Shakespeare begins his play at the beginning of the story, or near it. The subsequent developments of plot and situation are then shown, successively, in the stage action. This happens in Macbeth, for example. The play opens with the onset of ambition in Macbeth's mind, and the rest of the action charts the disastrous consequences of this ambition. The advantage of this method is that it makes long pauses for exposition unnecessary. The audience knows all it needs to know from the beginning. The drawback of the method lies in the fact that it often forces the playwright to get over long lapses of time (sometimes many years, as in The Winter's Tale), or changes of scene (as in the English episode in Macbeth), which are not themselves very dramatic. Shakespeare uses the opposite construction in The Tempest. The play opens near the end of the sequence of events. This requires a good deal of exposition, so that the audience will be aware of the events that lead to the situation in the stage. All of this exposition is given to Prospero in this scene. In the hands of a lesser playwright this might degenerate into the dullest kind of stage-talk. Shakespeare is careful to introduce various devices—Prospero's periodic reminders to Miranda to be attentive, his own flashes of anger as he recalls the story, the drama of the story itself—to keep the dramatic tension alive.

The transition from Miranda's concern over the fate of the mariners in the tempest to Prospero's story is subtly made at 18-23. When Prospero reminds his daughter that she does not really know who he is, he excites the interest of the audience in his mystery. He is obviously someone of note, and possessed of magical powers, yet he is only "the master

She said thou wast my daughter; and thy father
Was Duke of Milan; and his only heir
A princess — no worse issued.
    Miranda.   O the heavens!   59
What foul play had we that we came from thence?
Or blessed was't we did?
    Prospero.   Both, both, my girl!
By foul play, as thou say'st, were we heaved thence,
But blessedly holp hither.
    Miranda.   O, my heart bleeds   63
To think o' th' teen that I have turned you to,   64
Which is from my remembrance! Please you, farther.   65
    Prospero. My . brother and thy uncle, called
      Antonio —
I pray thee mark me — that a brother should
Be so perfidious! — he whom next thyself
Of all the world I loved, and to him put   69
The manage of my state, as at that time   70
Through all the signories it was the first   71
And Prospero the prime duke, being so reputed
In dignity, and for the liberal arts
Without a parallel; those being all my study,
The government I cast upon my brother
And to my state grew stranger, being transported   76
And rapt in secret studies. Thy false uncle —   77
Dost thou attend me?
    Miranda.   Sir, most heedfully.
    Prospero. Being once perfected how to grant suits,   79
How to deny them, who t' advance, and who
To trash for over-topping, new-created   81
The creatures that were mine, I say, or changed 'em,
Or else new-formed 'em; having both the key   83
Of officer and office, set all hearts i' th' state
To what tune pleased his ear, that now he was
The ivy which had hid my princely trunk
And sucked my verdure out on't. Thou attend'st
    not?   87
    Miranda. O, good sir, I do.
    Prospero.   I pray thee mark me.
I thus neglecting worldly ends, all dedicated   89
To closeness, and the bettering of my mind   90
With that which, but by being so retired,
O'er-prized all popular rate, in my false brother   92
Awaked an evil nature, and my trust,
Like a good parent, did beget of him
A falsehood in its contrary as great
As my trust was, which had indeed no limit,
A confidence sans bound. He being thus lorded   97
Not only with what my revenue yielded
But what my power might else exact, like one
Who having unto truth, by telling of it,   100
Made such a sinner of his memory
To credit his own lie, he did believe
He was indeed the Duke, out o' th' substitution   103
And executing th' outward face of royalty
With all prerogative. Hence his ambition growing—
Dost thou hear?
    Miranda.   Your tale, sir, would cure deafness.
    Prospero. To have no screen between this part he
    played   107

59. "no worse issued": of no lower parentage.

63. "holp": helped.
64. "teen": pain.
    "turned you to": reminded you of.
65. "from my remembrance": not in my memory.

69-70. "and to him . . . state": and gave him the control of my state.

71. "signories": Italian states (those subject to a signior, or lord).

76. "And to . . . stranger": i.e., withdrew from my position as head of the state.
77. "rapt": absorbed.

79. "perfected": grown skillful in.

81. "trash for over-topping": check for being too bold.
    "new-created": i.e., transformed my supporters into his.
83. "key": the word is suggested by key of office, then leads, by its musical association, to "tune".

87. "verdure": vitality, health; the ivy is here parasitic.
89-97. The exact meaning of this speech has occasioned much debate. The editor of the Arden edition gives this paraphrase: "The fact of my retirement, in which I neglected worldly affairs and dedicated myself to secret studies of a kind beyond the understanding and esteem of the people, brought out a bad side of my brother's nature. Consequently the great, indeed boundless, trust I placed in him gave rise to a disloyalty equally great on his part, just as it sometimes happens that a father distinguished for virtue has a vicious son."
90. "closeness": secret (studies).
92. "O'er-prized": outvalued.
97. "sans": without.
    "lorded": made lord of.
100-103. "Who having . . . Duke": i.e., who by often telling a lie made his memory such a sinner against truth, that he came to believe the lie he told, that he was in fact the Duke.
103. "out": as a result.
107. "To have . . . Milan": i.e., in order to make himself the Duke in name as well as power.

THE TEMPEST

ACT I SCENE II

of a full poor cell" on a remote island. With "'Tis time I should inform thee further" Shakespeare has his audience as ready as Miranda to hear the story Prospero tells.

We learn much more than the bare facts of the story in Prospero's account. The innocence and purity that characterize Miranda are the result of a life lived outside the complications and sophistications of society. Milan and her once exalted position are "rather like a dream than an assurance." This remoteness from the concerns of society is necessary for Miranda's function in the play. Her love for Ferdinand is uncomplicated and immediate; he is one of the "beauteous creatures" of the "brave new world." By the same token she is unable to understand the evil of an Antonio. Her admirable but naive innocence is balanced by Prospero's knowledge.

At 66 Prospero's story ceases to be simply a recollection of the past. He is moved to anger at the memory of his brother's perfidy. This surge of something close to rage has two effects: (1) It gives reality and emotional force to the recital of events that are twelve years old, giving them a present existence on the stage. (2) It indicates the evil disposition of some of the members of the court party, Antonio in particular. We have already received some suggestion in I.i. of Antonio's inhumanity. Now it is confirmed in the story of his treachery. In a general way it may be said that evil appears in The Tempest in two forms: in the bestiality of Caliban beneath human reason and morality, in the wickedness of Antonio and Sebastian which is worse, since it is the perversion of human reason and morality.

And him he played it for, he needs will be
Absolute Milan. Me (poor man) my library   109
Was dukedom large enough. Of temporal royalties   110
He thinks me now incapable; confederates   111
(So dry he was for sway) with th' King of Naples   112
To give him annual tribute, do him homage,
Subject his coronet to his crown, and bend   114
The dukedom yet unbowed (alas, poor Milan!)
To most ignoble stooping.
    Miranda.   O the heavens!
    Prospero. Mark his condition, and th' event; then
      tell me   117
If this might be a brother.
    Miranda.   I should sin
To think but nobly of my grandmother.   119
Good wombs have borne bad sons.
    Prospero.   Now the condition.
This King of Naples, being an enemy
To me inveterate, hearkens my brother's suit;
Which was, that he, in lieu o' th' premises   123
Of homage and I know not how much tribute,
Should presently extirpate me and mine   125
Out of the dukedom and confer fair Milan,
With all the honors, on my brother. Whereon,
A treacherous army levied, one midnight
Fated to th' purpose, did Antonio open   129
The gates of Milan; and, i' th' dead of darkness,
The ministers for th' purpose hurried thence   131
Me and thy crying self.
    Miranda.   Alack, for pity!
I, not rememb'ring how I cried out then,
Will cry it o'er again; it is a hint   134
That wrings mine eyes to't.
    Prospero.   Hear a little further, 135
And then I'll bring thee to the present business
Which now's upon's; without the which this story
Were most impertinent.
    Miranda.   Wherefore did they not 138
That hour destroy us?
    Prospero.   Well demanded, wench.
My tale provokes that question. Dear, they durst
    not,
So dear the love my people bore me; nor set
A mark so bloody on the business; but
With colors fairer painted their foul ends.
In few, they hurried us aboard a bark,   144
Bore us some leagues to sea; where they prepared
A rotten carcass of a butt, not rigged,   146
Nor tackle, sail, nor mast; the very rats
Instinctively have quit it. There they hoist us,
To cry to th' sea that roared to us; to sigh
To th' winds, whose pity, sighing back again,
Did us but loving wrong.
    Miranda.   Alack, what trouble
Was I then to you!
    Prospero.   O, a cherubin
Thou wast that did preserve me! Thou didst smile,
Infused with a fortitude from heaven,
When I have decked the sea with drops full salt,
Under my burden groaned; which raised in me   156

109. "Absolute Milan": the Duke of Milan in every sense; Milan is pronounced throughout with the accent on the first syllable.

110. "temporal royalties": the rule of temporary, material things (as opposed to intellectual studies).

111. "confederates": joins with.

112. "dry": thirsty, eager.

114. "his coronet . . . his crown": the rule of Milan, the kingdom of Naples.

117. "condition": agreement. "event": outcome.

119. "but": otherwise than.

123. "in lieu . . . premises": i.e., in return for Antonio's undertaking to pay homage and tribute, Alonso was to "extirpate" Prospero.

125. "presently": immediately.

129. "Fated": dedicated.

131. "ministers": agents.

134. "hint": occasion.

135. "wrings": forces.

138. "impertinent": not to the purpose (opposite of 'pertinent').

144. "In few": in brief.

146. "butt": barrel, tub.

156. "which": Miranda's smile.

THE TEMPEST

ACT I SCENE II

In Shakespeare's last plays, his romances, the ending is always a happy one. The romances recall the great tragedies in that there is always some force for evil or potential tragedy at work in them. Antonio, in II.i, bears a great resemblance to such evil figures in the tragedies as Iago, Edmund, and Lady Macbeth—figures through whom, or in whom, evil does triumph. The story which Prospero tells might be regarded as a tragic one, with Prospero as its ill-fated hero. Like the tragic heros proper he is a great man, "the prime duke, being so reputed/ In dignity, and for the liberal arts/ Without a parallel." Like the tragic heroes Prospero has a flaw, or weakness, which is the exaggeration of one of his virtues, the desire for knowledge. He grows a "stranger" to the state he governs, "being transported/ And rapt in secret studies." Shakespeare carefully elaborates the details of Prospero's situation, since they have a bearing on Prospero's present knowledge of human nature, which surpasses anyone else's in the play. Prospero's fault was in "neglecting worldly ends" in favor of "the bettering of my mind." Such dedication may be admirable, but it had the effect of betraying Prospero to his enemies, who were solely dedicated to the worldly ends of power. In the typical tragic situation the hero misunderstands his position. He acts so as to produce his own destruction, and this is exactly what Prospero did. But of course The Tempest is not a tragedy. The reason for the detailed inclusion of the Prospero-story is to show us a man who, like the tragic hero, has brought suffering on himself. Unlike the tragic hero, he is able to survive and benefit from the knowledge earned from suffering. The elements of Shakespeare's great tragic period are still components of the last romances.

An undergoing stomach, to bear up   157
Against what should ensue.
    Miranda.   How came we ashore?
    Prospero. By providence divine.
Some food we had, and some fresh water, that
A noble Neapolitan, Gonzalo,
Out of his charity, who being then appointed
Master of this design, did give us, with
Rich garments, linens, stuffs, and necessaries
Which since have steaded much. So, of his gentle-
       ness,   165
Knowing I loved my books, he furnished me
From mine own library with volumes that
I prize above my dukedom.
    Miranda.   Would I might
But ever see that man!
    Prospero.   Now I arise.   169
Sit still, and hear the last of our sea-sorrow.
Here in this island we arrived; and here
Have I, thy schoolmaster, made thee more profit   172
Than other princess can, that have more time   173
For vainer hours, and tutors not so careful.
    Miranda. Heavens thank you for't! And now I pray
       you, sir, —
For still 'tis beating in my mind, — your reason
For raising this sea-storm?
    Prospero.   Know thus far forth.
By accident most strange, bountiful Fortune
(Now my dear lady) hath mine enemies
Brought to this shore; and by my prescience
I find my zenith doth depend upon   181
A most auspicious star, whose influence   182
If now I court not, but omit, my fortunes   183
Will ever after droop. Here cease more questions.
Thou art inclined to sleep. 'Tis a good dullness,   185
And give it way. I know thou canst not choose.
                   [MIRANDA *sleeps.*
Come away, servant, come! I am ready now.   187
Approach, my Ariel: come!

       Enter ARIEL.

    Ariel. All hail, great master! Grave sir, hail! I
       come
To answer thy best pleasure; be't to fly,
To swim, to dive into the fire, to ride
On the curled clouds. To thy strong bidding task   192
Ariel and all his quality.
    Prospero.   Hast thou, spirit,   193
Performed to point the tempest that I bade thee?   194
    Ariel. To every article.
I boarded the King's ship: now on the beak,   196
Now in the waist, the deck, in every cabin,
I flamed amazement: sometime I'ld divide
And burn in many places; on the topmast,
The yards, and boresprit would I flame distinctly,   200
Then meet and join. Jove's lightnings, the precursors
O' th' dreadful thunderclaps, more momentary
And sight-outrunning were not. The fire and cracks
Of sulphurous roaring the most mighty Neptune
Seem to besiege and make his bold waves tremble;

Foreshadowing

157. "undergoing stomach": enduring spirit.

165. "steaded much": stood us in good stead.

169. "Now I arise": Prospero here resumes his magic robe to put Miranda to sleep, and summon Ariel.

172. "more profit": profit more.

173. "princess": plural understood.

181. "my zenith": the high point of my fortune.

182. "influence": in the astrological sense.

183. "omit": neglect.

185. "good dullness": i.e., this disposition to sleep is good.

187. "come away": come here.

192. "task": put to work

193. "quality": those spirits like him.

194. "to point": in every detail.

196. "beak": bow.

200. "boresprit": bowsprit.
"flame distinctly": burn in several places.

THE TEMPEST

ACT I SCENE II

At the end of his story Miranda asks Prospero the question that would arise naturally in the minds of the audience: "I pray you sir . . . Your reason for raising this sea-storm?" His answer, that Fortune brought his enemies to this shore prepares us for the main action of the play itself. The storm is the first event in the working-out of a deliberate plan, which will test the individuals who have landed on the magic island in various ways. What this plan is the audience does not know, but their sense of its existence intensifies their anticipation for what is to come.

2. Prospero has put off his robe during his recollection of the past, and on taking it up again at 169, he resumes the character of a magician. His first magical act is to put Miranda to sleep (sleep is a frequent dramatic device in the play). His next is to summon his servant-spirit, Ariel. For the Elizabethans, magicians might be of two kinds. There was the "black" magician, who could control the elements, but did so for evil ends. The witch Sycorax, Caliban's mother, with her "mischiefs manifold and sorceries terrible" was an example of this type. There was also the magician adept at "white" magic. Prospero was a "white" magician. The fact that the superstitions of some elements of the Elizabethan audience have long been discredited makes no difference to the imaginative effect of the magic in the play. It is one of the conventions of a romance, like The Tempest, that in its plot all the ordinary laws of causality are suspended. Here the suspension takes the form of Prospero's spirits, and his manipulation of the people and events on the island.

Yea, his dread trident shake.

Prospero.   My brave spirit!
Who was so firm, so constant, that this coil   207
Would not infect his reason?

Ariel.   Not a soul
But felt a fever of the mad and played   209
Some tricks of desperation. All but mariners
Plunged in the foaming brine and quit the vessel;
Then all afire with me the King's son Ferdinand,
With hair up-staring (then like reeds, not hair),   213
Was the first man that leapt; cried "Hell is empty,
And all the devils are here!"

Prospero.   Why, that's my spirit!
But was not this nigh shore?

Ariel.   Close by, my master.

Prospero. But are they, Ariel, safe?

Ariel.   Not a hair perished.
On their sustaining garments not a blemish,   218
But fresher than before; and as thou bad'st me,
In troops I have dispersed them 'bout the isle.
The King's son have I landed by himself,
Whom I left cooling of the air with sighs
In an odd angle of the isle, and sitting,
His arms in this sad knot.

Prospero.   Of the King's ship   224
The mariners say how thou hast disposed,
And all the rest o' th' fleet.

Ariel.   Safely in harbor
Is the King's ship; in the deep nook where once
Thou call'dst me up at midnight to fetch dew
From the still-vexed Bermoothes, there she's hid;   229
The mariners all under hatches stowed,
Who, with a charm joined to their suff'red labor,   231
I have left asleep; and for the rest o' th' fleet,
Which I dispersed, they all have met again,
And are upon the Mediterranean flote   234
Bound sadly home for Naples,
Supposing that they saw the King's ship wracked
And his great person perish.

Prospero.   Ariel, thy charge
Exactly is performed; but there's more work.
What is the time o' th' day?

Ariel.   Past the mid season.   239

Prospero. At least two glasses. The time 'twixt six
         and now   240
Must by us both be spent most preciously.

Ariel. Is there more toil? Since thou dost give me
         pains,
Let me remember thee what thou hast promised,
Which is not yet performed me.

Prospero.   How now? moody?
What is't thou canst demand?

Ariel.   My liberty.

Prospero. Before the time be out? No more!

Ariel.   I prithee,   246
Remember I have done thee worthy service,
Told thee no lies, made no mistakings, served
Without or grudge or grumblings. Thou did promise
To bate me a full year.

Prospero.   Dost thou forget   250

207. "coil": turmoil, uproar.

209. "of the mad": such as the mad feel.

213. "up-staring": standing straight up.

218. "sustaining": keeping them afloat.

224. "this sad knot": Ariel folds his arms by way of illustration.

229. "still-vexed Bermoothes": the continually stormy Bermudas; the spelling is an approximation of the Spanish pronunciation of the islands' proper name, Bermudez.

231. "suff'red labor": the work they have done.

234. "flote": flood, and hence also sea.

239. "mid season": noon.

240. "glasses": hour-glasses.

246. "time": allotted term of service.

250. "bate": abate, shorten.

THE TEMPEST

ACT I SCENE II

The spirit who is the chief instrument of Prospero's magic is Ariel. His first words associate him with "air" and "fire," which were for the Elizabethans the higher, rarefied elements of nature: opposed to them were earth and water (represented by Caliban). Ariel is not so much a character in his own right, as he is the representation of Prospero's art. In the speech at 195, for example, Ariel personifies the storm itself, who "flamed amazement" to the terrified mariners. At 220 we get a further suggestion as to the way in which Prospero's plot will work. We are told that Ariel has distributed the storm's survivors in various places about the island. They have been divided into (a) the King and the court party, (b) Ferdinand, and (c) Stephano and Trinculo. Each party will have their own purgative experiences to undergo before the play's end, to which each will respond characteristically and differently.

Where Ariel's poetry suggested the higher elements of air and fire, Caliban is associated with the lower, with water and earth, the "springs, brine-pits, barren place and fertile." Where Ariel rides "on the curled clouds," Caliban's habitat is "this hard rock" (usually represented in production as some sort of cave at the rear of the stage). Of Caliban's opening speech Mark van Doren has written: "We know Caliban first of all by his style, which gives us a creature complete in beastliness. His characteristic speech does not open the mouth to music; it closes it rather on harsh, hissing or guttural consonants that in the slowness with which they must be uttered express the difficult progress of a mind bemired in fact, an imagination beslimed with particulars. Caliban has no other capacity for abstraction, and consequently for the rational harmonies of music and love. The second of these

From what a torment I did free thee?
  Ariel.   No.
  Prospero. Thou dost; and think'st it much to tread the ooze
Of the salt deep,
To run upon the sharp wind of the North,
To do me business in the veins o' th' earth   255
When it is baked with frost.
  Ariel.   I do not, sir.
  Prospero. Thou liest, malignant thing! Hast thou forgot
The foul witch Sycorax, who with age and envy   258
Was grown into a hoop? Hast thou forgot her?
  Ariel. No, sir.
  Prospero.   Thou hast. Where was she born?
    Speak! Tell me!
  Ariel.   Sir, in Argier.
  Prospero.   O, was she so? I must   261
Once in a month recount what thou hast been,
Which thou forget'st. This damned witch Sycorax,
For mischiefs manifold, and sorceries terrible
To enter human hearing, from Argier,
Thou know'st, was banished. For one thing she did 266
They would not take her life. Is not this true?
  Ariel. Ay, sir.
  Prospero. This blue-eyed hag was hither brought with child
And here was left by th' sailors. Thou, my slave,
As thou report'st thyself, wast then her servant;
And, for thou wast a spirit too delicate
To act her earthy and abhorred commands,
Refusing her grand hests, she did confine thee,   274
By help of her more potent ministers,
And in her most unmitigable rage,
Into a cloven pine; within which rift
Imprisoned thou didst painfully remain
A dozen years; within which space she died
And left thee there, where thou didst vent thy groans
As fast as millwheels strike. Then was this island 281
(Save for the son that she did litter here,
A freckled whelp, hag-born) not honored with
A human shape.
  Ariel.   Yes, Caliban her son.
  Prospero. Dull thing, I say so: he, that Caliban
Whom now I keep in service. Thou best know'st
What torment I did find thee in: thy groans
Did make wolves howl and penetrate the breasts
Of ever-angry bears. It was a torment
To lay upon the damned, which Sycorax
Could not again undo. It was mine art,
When I arrived and heard thee, that made gape
The pine, and let thee out.
  Ariel.   I thank thee, master.
  Prospero. If thou more murmur'st, I will rend an oak
And peg thee in his knotty entrails till
Thou hast howled away twelve winters.
  Ariel.   Pardon, master.
I will be correspondent to command   297
And do my spriting gently.

255. "veins": streams.

258. "Sycorax": the name is usually explained as a combination of the Greek words for sow (sys) and raven (korax); there may also be a connection with the classical witch Circe, whom Sycorax resembles in various ways.
"envy": hatred.

261. "Argier": Algiers.

266. "one thing she did": Sycorax was pregnant, and therefore exiled instead of executed.

274. "hests": commands.

281. "millwheels": the paddles of a millwheel.

297. "correspondent": obedient.

THE TEMPEST

ACT I SCENE II

sentences (324) is scarcely articulated; it is a mouthed curse which no tongue's skill can refine." Caliban and Ariel exist at opposite ends of the spectrum of animal creation. Ariel is beyond humanity at the superhuman or spiritual end of the scale. Caliban is beneath humanity at the animal end. Caliban, combining animality and humanity, is one of the significant characters in the play (see below for a discussion of Caliban and Montaigne's "cannibal"). His heritage, given by Prospero at 319-20, indicates all that is evil and perverse. The references made to him by the rest of the characters, especially Stephano and Trinculo, are to a "monster", something indescribable between a land and sea-animal. As van Doren suggests, Caliban's language is evocative of all that is material, brutal and coarse. Yet Shakespeare's characterizations are never quite this simple, especially not in this subtle and complex play. There are times when Caliban's language becomes as exalted and lyrical (see especially III.ii.140), as any given to Ariel or Prospero. Even in the present scene, where the main purpose is to present the bestial Caliban, there are at least two touches which to some extent qualify the notion of "monster". The first comes at 333, where Caliban recalls the love that Prospero once showed him, and the way in which Prospero's gift of rational knowledge (here represented by the naming of the sun and moon) was repaid by Caliban's instinctive, natural knowledge of the island's properties. There is an attractive quality about this early association of the two outcasts. It was broken, Prospero then reveals, by Caliban's attempted assault upon Miranda. The implication is that the natural, instinctive creature may have an attractive innocence but will behave naturally and instinctively—that is without any of the controls of social or moral order. Caliban is then denounced (by Miranda, although some editors give this speech at 351-62 to Prospero) as "a thing most brutish." The attempt by Prospero-Miranda to teach Caliban to talk coherently produces the second affecting note in the portrayal of Caliban. It is a sentence of Caliban's which is typically Shakespearean in its brevity and compressing meaning: "You taught me language, and my profit on't/ Is, I know how to curse." These lines have often been applied to the European conquest and suppression of primitive, native peoples in Africa and the New World, that was beginning in Shakespeare's day.

Prospero.   Do so; and after two days   298
I will discharge thee.
    Ariel.   That's my noble master!
What shall I do? Say what? What shall I do?
    Prospero.   Go make thyself like a nymph o' th'
        sea. Be subject
To no sight but thine and mine; invisible
To every eyeball else. Go take this shape
And hither come in't. Go! Hence with diligence!
                    [*Exit* ARIEL.
Awake, dear heart, awake! Thou hast slept well.
Awake!
    Miranda.   The strangeness of your story put
Heaviness in me.
    Prospero.   Shake it off. Come on.
We'll visit Caliban, my slave, who never
Yields us kind answer.
    Miranda.   'Tis a villain, sir,
I do not love to look on.
    Prospero.   But as 'tis,
We cannot miss him: he does make our fire,   311
Fetch in our wood, and serves in offices
That profit us. What, ho! slave! Caliban!
Thou earth, thou! Speak!
    Caliban. [*within*]   There's wood enough within.
    Prospero. Come forth, I say! There's other business for thee.
Come, thou tortoise! When?   316

        Enter ARIEL *like a water nymph.*

Fine apparition! My quaint Ariel,   317
Hark in thine ear.
    Ariel.   My lord, it shall be done. [*Exit.*
    Prospero. Thou poisonous slave, got by the devil
        himself
Upon thy wicked dam, come forth!

           Enter CALIBAN.

Caliban. As wicked dew as e'er my mother brushed
With raven's feather from unwholesome fen
Drop on you both! A south-west blow on ye   323
And blister you all o'er!
    Prospero. For this, be sure, tonight thou shalt
        have cramps,
Side-stitches that shall pen thy breath up; urchins   326
Shall, for that vast of night that they may work,   327
All exercise on thee; thou shalt be pinched   328
As thick as honeycomb, each pinch more stinging
Than bees that made 'em.
    Caliban.   I must eat my dinner.
This island's mine by Sycorax my mother,
Which thou tak'st from me. When thou cam'st first,
Thou strok'st me and made much of me; wouldst
        give me
Water with berries in't; and teach me how
To name the bigger light, and how the less,   335
That burn by day and night; and then I loved thee
And showed thee all the qualities o' th' isle,   337
The fresh springs, brine-pits, barren place and
        fertile.

298. "And do . . . gently": do my work as a spirit graciously.

311. "miss": do without; the suggestion is that Caliban, despite his bestiality, is somehow necessary to the human condition.

316. "When?": i.e., when are you coming? an expression of impatience.

317. "quaint": the word has various Elizabethan meanings: skillful, ingenious, delicate, elegant.

323. "A south-west": frequently mentioned as an unhealthy wind.

326. "pen": the word combines the meanings of 'to pen up' (enclose tightly) and 'to pin' (jab painfully). "urchins": hedgehogs, or malicious spirits who assumed their shape.

327. "vast": void or waste (*Hamlet*, I.ii.198, "In the dead vast and middle of the night").

328. "All exercise": i.e., all their habitual activity.

335. "the bigger light": the sun. "the less": the moon.

337. "qualities": the resources.

THE TEMPEST

ACT I SCENE II

In the colonizing process, it is pointed out, natives are invariably introduced to the worst elements in the colonizers' civilization. A native population exposed to an occupying army seems always to learn the visitors' obscenities before any of the other elements of their language. In the case of *The Tempest*, the colonizing analogy is not so much with the Prospero-Caliban relationship as it is with the perversely 'civilized' influence of the Europeans Stephano and Trinculo on the "servant-monster" at II.ii. The character of Caliban has a certain pathos throughout the play. It is first felt in this scene, in his failure to comprehend Prospero's language (i.e., knowledge) for any but base purposes.

3. Ariel enters at 374, invisible (see glossary, SD), and sings two of Shakespeare's most beautiful songs. Songs in Shakespeare's plays do not occur simply as a variation from dramatic speech or to provide an interlude of lute playing. They have also a more organic function. Songs reflect and intensify the prevailing mood of the scene or situation. Sometimes, as in Ariel's second song here, they give lyrical statement to some underlying theme of the whole play.

Cursed be I that did so! All the charms
Of Sycorax — toads, beetles, bats, light on you!
For I am all the subjects that you have,
Which first was mine own king; and here you sty me   342
In this hard rock, whiles you do keep from me
The rest o' th' island.
   Prospero.   Thou most lying slave,
Whom stripes may move, not kindness! I have used
   thee   345
(Filth as thou art) with humane care, and lodged
   thee
In mine own cell till thou didst seek to violate
The honor of my child.
   Caliban. O ho, O ho! Would't had been done!
Thou didst prevent me; I had peopled else
This isle with Calibans.
   Miranda.   Abhorred slave,   351
Which any print of goodness wilt not take,   352
Being capable of all ill! I pitied thee,
Took pains to make thee speak, taught thee each
   hour
One thing or other: when thou didst not, savage,
Know thine own meaning, but wouldst gabble like
A thing most brutish, I endowed thy purposes
With words that made them known. But thy vile
   race,   358
Though thou didst learn, had that in't which good
   natures   359
Could not abide to be with; therefore wast thou
Deservedly confined into this rock, who hadst
Deserved more than a prison.
   Caliban. You taught me language, and my profit
   on't
Is, I know how to curse. The red plague rid you   364
For learning me your language!
   Prospero.   Hag-seed, hence!
Fetch us in fuel; and be quick, thou'rt best,   366
To answer other business. Shrug'st thou, malice   367
If thou neglect'st or dost unwillingly
What I command, I'll rack thee with old cramps,   369
Fill all thy bones with aches, make thee roar
That beasts shall tremble at thy din.
   Caliban.   No, pray thee.
[*Aside*] I must obey. His art is of such pow'r
It would control my dam's god, Setebos,   373
And make a vassal of him.
   Prospero.   So, slave; hence! [*Exit* CALIBAN.

Enter FERDINAND; *and* ARIEL (*invisible*), *playing and*
   singing.   SD

      Ariel's song.

Come unto these yellow sands,
   And then take hands.
Curtsied when you have and kissed,
   The wild waves whist,   378
Foot it featly here and there;   379
And, sweet sprites, the burden bear.   380
   Hark, hark!

[handwritten margin note:] — monster + brute

---

342. "sty": imprison, as in a sty.

345. "stripes": lashes of a whip.

351. "Abhorred slave . . .": some editors have given this speech to Prospero, on the grounds that the gentle Miranda would not speak with this vehemence and power. However, as a recent editor has said, "Miranda is outraged, with the anger proper to a just person in the face of evil."

352. "print of goodness": education in morality.

358. "race": inherited nature.

359. "good natures": natural virtues.

364. "red plague": bubonic plague. "rid": destroy.

366. "thou'rt best": it were best for you.

367. "malice": Caliban is addressed as malice personified.

369. "old cramps": the cramps that afflict the old.

373. "Setebos": a god of the Patagonians; Shakespeare may have come across the name in an account of Magellan's voyages.

SD. "Ariel invisible": Elizabethan theatrical costumes included "a gown for to go invisible," which Ariel would wear here; the Japanese theater still uses conventionally invisible costumes.

378. "whist": being stilled.

379. "featly": nimbly.

380. "burden": refrain, or chorus; here, the animal noises.

THE TEMPEST

ACT I SCENE II

Ariel leads Ferdinand onto and across the stage with his first song. Ferdinand realizes that he is being worked on by some supernatural power which allays both the fury of the storm, and his own grief for his father. In following the storm with music Shakespeare uses two symbols which recur frequently in his plays: storm as disorder, disharmony and destruction; music as harmony and serenity. Ariel's appearances vary with the character of the person to whom he appears. Ferdinand does not share Antonio's or Alonso's guilt. Ariel's songs are of reassurance and comfort. Both the songs are of beautiful lyric simplicity but, as so often in Shakespeare, they carry meanings that are neither superficial nor simple. The first song is an invitation to dance by the sea. As Ferdinand dimly realizes, the "fury" of the sea is replaced by the harmony of the sweet air. The spirits who sing the refrain, or burden," are given the sounds of animals—but they are animals friendly to man, the domesticated dog and rooster. In one sense these animal sounds represent the voice of nature, but now, after the storm, it is a nature that is friendly, and in which man has a place. The second song is more specific in its reference, as Ferdinand sees: "The ditty does remember my drowned father." It is one of the loveliest of Shakespeare's songs and perhaps because it is, its significance is often overlooked. Ferdinand has been mourning the supposed death of his father. The song does not bother to deny the drowning, but speaks of it as a "sea-change" rather than as a death. The imagery of the coral and pearls suggest a new richness and value, a metamorphosis "into something rich and strange." The implication is that Ferdinand is not to lament his father's death. The storm has, in some mysterious way, produced a new and better being. Again, "Though the seas threaten, they are merciful," Ferdinand is not to realize the truth of this completely until V.i. In one sense the whole concern of the play is with the changes that the various characters undergo during their sojourn on the island. Those characters who have potential virtue within them achieve it. Ferdinand's father is one of these as is made clear at III.ii. where he realizes and suffers for his guilt. It is this possibility of a transformation for the better that is mysteriously hinted at in Ariel's song. What seems to be death ("Full fathom five thy father lies") will turn out to be a new and better life ("something rich and strange").

[Burden, dispersedly.] Bowgh, wawgh! SD
The watchdogs bark.
   [Burden, dispersedly.] Bowgh, wawgh!
Hark, hark! I hear
   The strain of strutting chanticleer
     Cry cock-a-diddle-dowe.

Ferdinand. Where should this music be? I' th' air
   or th' earth?
It sounds no more; and sure it waits upon
Some god o' th' island. Sitting on a bank,
Weeping again the King my father's wrack.
This music crept by me upon the waters,
Allaying both their fury and my passion 393
With its sweet air. Thence I have followed it,
Or it hath drawn me rather; but 'tis gone.
No, it begins again.

       Ariel's song.

  Full fathom five thy father lies;
    Of his bones are coral made;
  Those are pearls that were his eyes;
    Nothing of him that doth fade 400
  But doth suffer a sea-change
  Into something rich and strange.
  Sea nymphs hourly ring his knell:
      [Burden.] Dong-dong.
Hark! now I hear them — Ding-dong bell.

Ferdinand. The ditty does remember my drowned
   father. 406
This is no mortal business, nor no sound
That the earth owes. I hear it now above me. 408
Prospero. The fringed curtains of thine eye advance 409
And say what thou seest yond.
Miranda.   What is't? a spirit?
Lord, how it looks about! Believe me, sir,
It carries a brave form. But 'tis a spirit.
Prospero. No, wench: it eats, and sleeps, and hath
   such senses
As we have, such. This gallant which thou seest
Was in the wrack; and, but he's something stained 415
With grief (that's beauty's canker), thou mightst
   call him
A goodly person. He hath lost his fellows
And strays about to find 'em.
Miranda.   I might call him
A thing divine; for nothing natural 419
I ever saw so noble.
Prospero.   *[aside]* It goes on, I see, 420
As my soul prompts it. Spirit, fine spirit, I'll free
   thee
Within two days for this.
Ferdinand.   Most sure, the goddess 422
On whom these airs attend! Vouchsafe my prayer 423
May know if you remain upon this island, 424
And that you will some good instruction give
How I may bear me here. My prime request,
Which I do last pronounce, is (O you wonder!) 427
If you be maid or no?

SD. "Burden, dispersedly": perhaps from various singers offstage.

393. "my passion": i.e., of lament for his father.

400. "Nothing of him . . . But": i.e., all of him that decays is also transformed.

406. "does remember": commemorates.

408. "owes": owns, produces.

409. "fringed curtains . . . advance": i.e., raise your eyelids; Coleridge has pointed out that the elaborate, formal language here is appropriate to the solemnity of the moment: the introduction of Miranda to Ferdinand, and to the love which atones for the evils of the past.

415. "but": except that. "stained": disfigured.

419. "natural": from the world of nature, as opposed to the world of spirit.

420. "It goes on": i.e., the plan works as I had intended.

422. "Most sure": certainly this must be.

423. "these airs": the music Ferdinand has been following.

424. "remain upon": inhabit.

427. "O you wonder!": a play on Miranda's name (from the Latin *mirus*, wonderful) although Ferdinand does not yet know it.

THE TEMPEST

ACT I SCENE II

Ariel has led Ferdinand, as Prospero ordered, within sight of Miranda. It is part of Prospero's plan that the two fall in love and marry, thus healing the breach between Prospero and Alonso and, symbolically, showing the way in which love atones for and transcends strife and hatred. Their love is, of course, love at first sight. This is, in part, a necessary convention of the Elizabethan stage. Given the brief time in which a play must run its course, there was simply no room for an elaborate, realistic presentation of courting. But we must also recall that Ferdinand and Miranda are not meant to be "realistic" or naturalistic, lifelike characters of the kind that appear on our stage. They represent youth, purity, and innocence (as opposed to the experience of Prospero, the animality of Caliban, and the conscious evil of Antonio). Their love is deliberately idealized. Notice the difference between Miranda's reaction to Ferdinand, and Prospero's. For the innocent girl Ferdinand is "a thing divine"; for the knowledgeable father, "it eats and sleeps," is "something stained," but (somewhat reluctantly) "thou mightst call him/ A goodly person." For Ferdinand, of course, Miranda is what Shakespeare's name for her implies, that which is admired and wondered at (427).

reverse psychology ↓

Miranda.   No wonder, sir,
But certainly a maid.
Ferdinand.   My language? Heavens!
I am the best of them that speak this speech,
Were I but where 'tis spoken.
Prospero.   How? the best?
What wert thou if the King of Naples heard thee?
Ferdinand. A single thing, as I am now, that
   wonders   433
To hear thee speak of Naples. He does hear me;   434
And that he does I weep. Myself am Naples,
Who with mine eyes, never since at ebb, beheld
The King my father wracked.
Miranda.   Alack, for mercy!
Ferdinand. Yes, faith, and all his lords, the Duke
   of Milan
And his brave son being twain.
Prospero.   [aside] The Duke of Milan 439
And his more braver daughter could control thee, 440
If now 'twere fit to do't. At the first sight
They have changed eyes. Delicate Ariel,   442
I'll set thee free for this. — A word, good sir.
I fear you have done yourself some wrong. A word! 444
Miranda. Why speaks my father so ungently? This
Is the third man that e'er I saw; the first
That e'er I sighed for. Pity move my father
To be inclined my way!
Ferdinand.   O, if a virgin,
And your affection not gone forth, I'll make you
The Queen of Naples.
Prospero.   Soft, sir! one word more.
[Aside] They are both in either's pow'rs. But this
   swift business
I must uneasy make, lest too light winning   452
Make the prize light. — One word more! I charge
   thee   453
That thou attend me. Thou dost here usurp
The name thou ow'st not, and hast put thyself   455
Upon this island as a spy, to win it
From me, the lord on't.
Ferdinand.   No, as I am a man!
Miranda. There's nothing ill can dwell in such a
   temple.   458
If the ill spirit have so fair a house,
Good things will strive to dwell with't.
Prospero.   Follow me. —
Speak not you for him; he's a traitor. — Come!
I'll manacle thy neck and feet together;
Sea water shalt thou drink; thy food shall be
The fresh-brook mussels, withered roots, and husks
Wherein the acorn cradled. Follow!
Ferdinand.   No.
I will resist such entertainment till
Mine enemy has more power.

[*He draws, and is charmed from moving.*   SD

Miranda.   O dear father,
Make not too rash a trial of him, for   468
He's gentle, and not fearful.

433. "single": a) single, b) weak.
434. "Naples": King of Naples.

439. "son": either Antonio's son (not elsewhere mentioned), or else "his" refers back to "Naples".
440. "control": oppose or contradict.
442. "changed eyes": fallen in love; the phrase, arising from the exchange of amorous glances, was a common Elizabethan one.
444. "I fear...wrong": politely ironical for 'you are mistaken'.

452-3. "light": a quibble; in the first line the word means, easy; in the next, undervalued.

455. "ow'st": ownest.

458. "in such a temple": a conventional Renaissance idea, ultimately derived from Plato, that the body reflects the soul's virtue.

SD. "charmed from moving": by a gesture from Prospero.

468. "trial": judgment.

THE TEMPEST

ACT I SCENE II

Commentators have frequently wondered at the harshness with which Prospero treats Ferdinand— "I'll manacle thy neck and feet together/ Sea water shalt thou drink." There are, in fact, several points in the play where Prospero is harsh to those about him. We must recall how carefully Shakespeare has underlined the fact that it was Prospero's earlier delinquence, as Duke, in just this sort of supervisory watchfulness that produced his downfall. Prospero had not dealt with the real world. To deal with it effectively is to be aware of the constant threat of an Antonio, or a Caliban, or even a prospective suitor. Unlike Miranda, Prospero does not have the uncritical, unquestioning love that comes from innocence. Again, the whole structure of the play calls for this treatment of Ferdinand. All those who are approaching Prospero's cell—the court party, Stephano and Trinculo, and Ferdinand—undergo some sort of test of ordeal. Ferdinand must become Prospero's servant, laboring to provide his wood even as Caliban does, in order to win Miranda. Even Ariel complains, from time to time, of his enforced servitude. Both Ariel and Ferdinand attain their objective in the end, and one of the meanings of the play is illustrated in this. The way to freedom and fulfillment is through labor, discipline, and servitude.

Prospero. What, I say,	469
My foot my tutor?—Put thy sword up, traitor!	470
Who mak'st a show but dar'st not strike, thy conscience	
Is so possessed with guilt. Come, from thy ward!	472
For I can here disarm thee with this stick	
And make thy weapon drop.	
Miranda. Beseech you, father!	
Prospero. Hence! Hang not on my garments.	
Miranda. Sir, have pity.	
I'll be his surety.	
Prospero. Silence! One word more	476
Shall make me chide thee, if not hate thee. What,	
An advocate for an impostor? Hush!	
Thou think'st there is no more such shapes as he,	
Having seen but him and Caliban. Foolish wench!	
To th' most of men this is a Caliban,	481
And they to him are angels.	
Miranda. My affections	482
Are then most humble. I have no ambition	
To see a goodlier man.	
Prospero. Come on, obey!	
Thy nerves are in their infancy again	485
And have no vigor in them.	
Ferdinand. So they are.	
My spirits, as in a dream, are all bound up.	
My father's loss, the weakness which I feel,	
The wrack of all my friends, nor this man's threats	
To whom I am subdued, are but light to me,	
Might I but through my prison once a day	
Behold this maid. All corners else o' th' earth	
Let liberty make use of. Space enough	493
Have I in such a prison.	
Prospero. [*aside*] It works. [*to* FERDINAND] Come on. —	
Thou hast done well, fine Ariel! [*to* FERDINAND] Follow me.	
[*To* ARIEL] Hark what thou else shalt do me.	
Miranda. Be of comfort	
My father's of a better nature, sir,	
Than he appears by speech. This is unwonted	
Which now came from him.	
Prospero. Thou shalt be as free	
As mountain winds; but then exactly do	500
All points of my command.	
Ariel. To th' syllable.	
Prospero. Come, follow. — Speak not for him.	502
[*Exeunt.*	

469. "gentle": of noble birth.
"fearful": either a) cowardly, or b) to be feared.

470. "My foot my tutor?": i.e., am I to be instructed by something beneath me?

472. "ward": the stance assumed by a fencer.

476. "surety": guarantee.

481. "to": compared to.

482. "affections": preference, inclination.

485. "nerves": sinews.

493. "Let liberty . . . of": i.e., let those who are free make use of.

500. "but then": but until then.

502. "Speak not . . .": addressed to Miranda, who tries again to intercede in Ferdinand's behalf.

THE TEMPEST

ACT II SCENE I

The opening of this scene further defines and differentiates the members of the court party. Gonzalo, the "honest old councilor," characteristically tries to comfort the King in the loss of his son, but Alonso will not be comforted. Gonzalo's speeches are constructed so as to show that, despite his goodness, he is also a garrulous old man. Once embarked on a subject, he is difficult to stop. Here, the well-meant sentiments and elaborate reference to all the other people who "have just our theme of woe" is hardly calculated to cheer up the King as he mourns for Ferdinand.

Most editors print the exchange between Sebastian and Antonio which begins at 10 as an aside, that is, as speech not heard by the other actors on the stage. In any case the actors must play the passage as though they were standing aloof, commenting from their sharper, more sophisticated intelligences on the meanderings of the old man. Of this dialogue Coleridge has written: "Shakespeare shows the tendency in bad men to indulge in scorn and contemptuous expressions, as a mode of getting rid of their own uneasy feelings of inferiority to the good, and also, by making the good ridiculous, of rendering the transition of others to wickedness easy. Shakespeare never puts habitual scorn into the mouths of other than bad men." The cynical insensitivity of Sebastian and Antonio is a preliminary to their plot against the King. Gonzalo may be misguided in the way in which he tries to comfort Alonzo, but it is an effort based on his own sense of the value of human life, and on hope. Sebastian and Antonio suggest, in the acid and destructive tone of their talk, the complete lack of any such value. Sebastian and Antonio emerge as more acute than the rest of the group. They are able to anticipate and make fun of what Gonzalo and Adrian say almost before it is said. As Coleridge suggests, this kind of competitive intelligence, that continually scores points off other people to demonstrate how stupid they are is always associated in Shakespeare with some sort of moral blindness or lack of real understanding.

ACT TWO, scene one

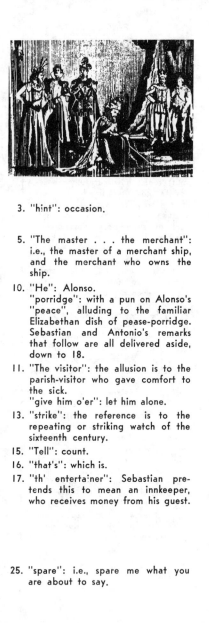

(ANOTHER PART OF THE ISLAND)

Enter ALONSO, SEBASTIAN, ANTONIO, GONZALO, ADRIAN, FRANCISCO, *and* Others.

Gonzalo. Beseech you, sir, be merry. You have cause
(So have we all) of joy; for our escape
Is much beyond our loss. Our hint of woe   3
Is common: every day some sailor's wife,
The master of some merchant, and the merchant,   5
Have just our theme of woe; but for the miracle,
I mean our preservation, few in millions
Can speak like us. Then wisely, good sir, weigh
Our sorrow with our comfort.
    Alonso.   Prithee peace.
Sebastian. He receives comfort like cold porridge.   10
Antonio. The visitor will not give him o'er so.   11
Sebastian. Look, he's winding up the watch of his
wit; by and by it will strike.   13
Gonzalo. Sir —
Sebastian. One. Tell.   15
Gonzalo. When every grief is entertained, that's
offered   16
Comes to th' entertainer —   17
Sebastian. A dollar.
Gonzalo. Dolor comes to him, indeed. You have
spoken truer than you purposed.
Sebastian. You have taken it wiselier than I meant
you should.
Gonzalo. Therefore, my lord —
Antonio. Fie, what a spendthrift is he of his tongue!
Alonso. I prithee spare.   25
Gonzalo. Well, I have done. But yet —
Sebastian. He will be talking.
Antonio. Which, of he or Adrian, for a good wager,
first begins to crow?
Sebastian. The old cock.   30
Antonio. The cock'rel.   31
Sebastian. Done! The wager?
Antonio. A laughter.   33
Sebastian. A match!
Adrian. Though this island seem to be desert —
Antonio. Ha, ha, ha!
Sebastian. So, you're paid.
Adrian. Uninhabitable and almost inaccessible —
Sebastian. Yet —
Adrian. Yet —
Antonio. He could not miss't.   41
Adrian. It must needs be of subtle, tender, and
delicate temperance.   43
Antonio. Temperance was a delicate wench.   44
Sebastian. Ay, and a subtle, as he most learnedly
delivered.
Adrian. The air breathes upon us here most sweetly.
Sebastian. As if it had lungs, and rotten ones.
Antonio. Or as 'twere perfumed by a fen.

---

3. "hint": occasion.

5. "The master . . . the merchant": i.e., the master of a merchant ship, and the merchant who owns the ship.

10. "He": Alonso.
"porridge": with a pun on Alonso's "peace", alluding to the familiar Elizabethan dish of pease-porridge. Sebastian and Antonio's remarks that follow are all delivered aside, down to 18.

11. "The visitor": the allusion is to the parish-visitor who gave comfort to the sick.
"give him o'er": let him alone.

13. "strike": the reference is to the repeating or striking watch of the sixteenth century.

15. "Tell": count.

16. "that's": which is.

17. "th' entertainer": Sebastian pretends this to mean an innkeeper, who receives money from his guest.

25. "spare": i.e., spare me what you are about to say.

30-1. "the old cock . . . the cock'rel": Gonzalo . . . Adrian.

33. "a laughter": i.e., the winner has the right to laugh.

41. "He could not miss't": ironic; however "inaccessible" the island, Adrian can manage to be shipwrecked on it.

43. "temperance": climate.

44. "Temperance": woman's proper name, often given by Puritans. Antonio suggests (probably with an indelicate wink) that he knew someone by that name.

36

THE TEMPEST

ACT II SCENE I

It is also noteworthy that the characters are defined by the attitude they take to their surroundings, by the way—literally—they see the island. When Adrian notices that "The air breathes upon us here most sweetly," Antonio counters with "as 'twere perfumed by a fen." Where Gonzalo finds the grass "lush and lusty . . . how green!" Antonio replies that it is "tawny." What matters is not the real state of the air or vegetation, but the contrast between the two kinds of perception; one responds to whatever is good; the other sees only the bad. It is Gonzalo who notices, what Ariel has already pointed out to the audience; that their clothes "drenched in the sea, hold, their freshness and gloss, being rather new-dyed than stained with salt water." This is not simply a matter of looking on the bright side. It is Gonzalo's fundamental goodness that makes him, rather than the others, aware of the miraculous nature of their salvation from the storm.

In the middle of the scene Gonzalo develops his fantasy concerning the "commonwealth" he would establish on the island. This seems at first to be a simple digression—perhaps another attempt to take the King's mind off his grief. The speech is relevant to one of the central themes of the play: civilization and society in contrast to nature and instinct. The debate between the relative merits of 'society' and 'nature' is at least as old as Plato. It was particularly relevant to the age of Shakespeare, when the voyages of discovery were continually revealing new worlds in which 'societies' of the kind Europe knew simply did not exist. Discoverers found people in what seemed to them to be a condition of primeval innocence —man in a state of nature, much as Adam was before the Fall.

Gonzalo. Here is everything advantageous to life.

Antonio. True; save means to live.

Sebastian. Of that there's none, or little.

Gonzalo. How lush and lusty the grass looks! how green!

Antonio. The ground indeed it tawny.   55

Sebastian. With an eye of green in't.   56

Antonio. He misses not much.

Sebastian. No; he doth but mistake the truth totally.

Gonzalo. But the rarity of it is — which is indeed almost beyond credit—

Sebastian. As many vouched rarities are.   62

Gonzalo. That our garments, being, as they were, drenched in the sea, hold, notwithstanding, their freshness and gloss, being rather new-dyed than stained with salt water.

Antonio. If but one of his pockets could speak, would it not say he lies?   67

Sebastian. Ay, or very falsely pocket up his report.

Gonzalo. Methinks our garments are now as fresh as when we put them on first in Afric, at the marriage of the King's fair daughter Claribel to the King of Tunis.

Sebastian. 'Twas a sweet marriage, and we prosper well in our return.   74   75

Adrian. Tunis was never graced before with such a paragon to their queen.

Gonzalo. Not since widow Dido's time.   78

Antonio. Widow? A pox o' that! How came that "widow" in? Widow Dido!

Sebastian. What if he had said "widower Aeneas" too? Good Lord, how you take it!

Adrian. "Widow Dido," said you? You make me study of that. She was of Carthage, not of Tunis.

Gonzalo. This Tunis, sir, was Carthage.

Adrian. Carthage?

Gonzalo. I assure you, Carthage.

Antonio. His word is more than the miraculous harp.   88

Sebastian. He hath raised the wall and houses too.

Antonio. What impossible matter will he make easy next?

Sebastian. I think he will carry this island home in his pocket and give it his son for an apple.

Antonio. And, sowing the kernels of it in the sea, bring forth more islands.

Gonzalo. Ay!

Antonio. Why, in good time.

Gonzalo. Sir, we were talking that our garments seem now as fresh as when we were at Tunis at the marriage of your daughter, who is now Queen.

Antonio. And the rarest that e'er came there.

Sebastian. Bate, I beseech you, widow Dido.   102

Antonio. O, widow Dido? Ay, widow Dido.

Gonzalo. Is not, sir, my doublet as fresh as the first day I wore it? I mean, in a sort.   105

Antonio. That "sort" was well fished for.   106

Gonzalo. When I wore it at your daughter's marriage.

55. "tawny": burned by the sun.

56. "eye": center, or spot.

62. "vouched rarities": wonders said to be true.

67. "If but . . . lies": i.e., if he examined himself (and his pockets) closely he would see his mistake.

74-75. "and we prosper": a continuation of the sour irony present in most of what Sebastian and Antonio say.

78. "widow Dido": Dido, a familiar classical figure to the Elizabethans, was usually thought of as the lover of Aeneas, not the widow (as she was) of Sychaeus; presumably this unfashionable mistake is the cause of Antonio's sophisticated laughter. This is followed by Gonzalo's confusion of Tunis and Carthage. The point of the whole passage is to show Antonio and Sebastian making fun of Gonzalo. He makes mistakes, and is a good man. They are technically correct, morally corrupt.

88. "miraculous harp": Amphion's harp, which raised the walls of Thebes.

102. "Bate": expecting; meant sarcastically.

105. "in a sort": more or less, comparatively.

106. "That . . . for": i.e., you are wise to qualify in it that way; again, meant sarcastically.

Montaigne, the French philosopher, had considered this question and his *Essais* is one of the books that Shakespeare seems to have read and reflected on. The particular essay which gives rise to several of the notions in *The Tempest* was the one entitled "Of Cannibals," where Montaigne considers and contrasts the formal society of the Old World with the newly discovered primitive groups of the New. Montaigne takes the view (which was in his day a minority one, but was to gain much wider acceptance in the nineteenth century) that society as it was known in Europe was in many ways an artificial and corrupting force; that the Indians or "savages" of the New World who lived outside of society, were purer and better for it. This view came to be known as the doctrine of "the noble savage." Montaigne's argument proceeds from the analogy between the artificially grown and the natural plant: "They [the Indians] are even savage, as we call those fruits wild, which nature of herself ... hath produced; whereas indeed those which ourselves have altered by our artificial devices, and diverted from this common order, we should rather term savage. In those are the true and most profitable virtues, and natural properties most lively and vigorous, which in these we have bastardized, applying them to the pleasure of our corrupted taste. And if notwithstanding, in divers fruits of those countries that were never tilled, we shall find that in respect of ours they are most excellent, and as delicate unto our taste; there is no reason, art should gain the point of honour of our great and puissant mother Nature."

Alonso. You cram these words into mine ears against | 109
The stomach of my sense. Would I had never | 110
Married my daughter there! for, coming thence,
My son is lost; and, in my rate, she too, | 112
Who is so far from Italy removed
I ne'er again shall see her. O thou mine heir
Of Naples and of Milan, what strange fish
Hath made his meal on thee?
Francisco. Sir, he may live.
I saw him beat the surges under him
And ride upon their backs. He trod the water,
Whose enmity he flung aside, and breasted
The surge most swol'n that met him. His bold head
'Bove the contentious waves he kept, and oared
Himself with his good arms in lusty stroke
To th' shore, that o'er his wave-worn basis bowed, | 123
As stooping to relieve him. I not doubt
He came alive to land.
Alonso. No, no, he's gone.
Sebastian. Sir, you may thank yourself for this great loss,
That would not bless our Europe with your daughter,
But rather loose her to an African, | 128
Where she, at least, is banished from your eye | 129
Who hath cause to wet the grief on't.
Alonso. Prithee peace. | 130
Sebastian. You were kneeled to and importuned otherwise
By all of us; and the fair soul herself
Weighed, between loathness and obedience, at | 133
Which end o' th' beam should bow. We have lost your son, | 134
I fear, for ever. Milan and Naples have
Moe widows in them of this business' making | 136
Than we bring men to comfort them:
The fault's your own.
Alonso. So is the dear'st o' th' loss. | 138
Gonzalo. My Lord Sebastian,
The truth you speak doth lack some gentleness,
And time to speak it in. You rub the sore | 141
When you should bring the plaster.
Sebastian. Very well.
Antonio. And most chirurgeonly. | 143
Gonzalo. It is foul weather in us all, good sir,
When you are cloudy.
Sebastian. Foul weather?
Antonio. Very foul.
Gonzalo. Had I plantation of this isle, my lord — | 146
Antonio. He'd sow't with nettle seed.
Sebastian. Or docks, or mallows,
Gonzalo. And were the king on't, what would I do?
Sebastian. Scape being drunk for want of wine. | 149
Gonzalo. I' th' commonwealth I would by contraries | 150
Execute all things; for no kind of traffic | 151
Would I admit; no name of magistrate;
Letters should not be known; riches, poverty, | 153
And use of service, none; contract, succession, | 154
Bourn, bound of land, tilth, vineyard, none; | 155
No use of metal, corn, or wine, or oil;

109-10. "against . . . sense": in opposition to my inclination or feeling.

112. "rate": opinion.

123. "that o'er . . . bowed": i.e., that leaned over its own base.

128. "loose her": mate her with.

129-130. "from your . . . on't": i.e., from you, who have cause to weep for her.

133-34. "Weighed . . . bow": i.e., Claribel was torn between dislikes of the marriage and obedience to her father.

136. "Moe": more.

138. "dear'st": most deeply felt.

141. "time": the suitable time.

143. "chirurgeonly": like a surgeon (with reference to "sore").

146. "plantation": the colonization, but Antonio chooses to understand the literal sense of sowing seed.

149. "Scape": escape, avoid.

150. "by contraries": in contrast to the usual practice.

151. "traffic": trade, commerce.

153. "Letters": written documents, particularly of ownership.

154. "use of service": practice of having servants.
"succession": inheritance.

155. "Bourn . . . land": establishment of limits of private property.

THE TEMPEST

ACT II SCENE I

This superiority of the natural over the artificial life lies behind Gonzalo's commonwealth, which is in a state of nature, without "traffic" (i.e., commerce) riches, poverty, or even any "sovereignty" of one man over another. In fact this passage has been cited as one of the earliest statements in imaginative literature of the idea of the value of primitivism (Gonzalo's "golden age"). That it is Gonzalo who expresses the idea is in itself significant. He is himself naturally innocent and good, and perhaps incapable of seeing the evil potential in the human animal. It is ironic that he speaks his vision of the perfect, natural, and uncontrolled society before Antonio and Sebastian, unaware that as long as predatory individuals such as they exist, his perfect society would rapidly become a jungle, red in tooth and claw.

Shakespeare has used Montaigne's essay in another way in his play. The name Caliban is an anagram of cannibal. Caliban is another argument against the possibility of an ideal, primitive society. In effect, Caliban is Prospero's experiment with Montaigne's idea of the noble savage, and it has been a failure. Caliban is one "on whose nature/ Nurture can never stick" (IV.i.188). This conflict between 'nature'— the instinctive basis of humanity— and 'nurture'—the control and elevation of the instinctive human animal through the civilizing effects of knowledge and education (in the widest sense) occurs throughout the play. Against Gonzalo's theory of primitive perfection, we have the practical argument of Caliban's unregenerate animality.

Ariel's music induces sleep in all the members of the court party except Sebastian and Antonio, leaving the way open for their plot to murder Antonio, a development that Shakespeare has prepared for by the earlier characterization of the two conspirators. The presence of Ariel and the magically induced sleep remind us that the conspiracy is contrived as a part of Prospero's plan, and that it cannot succeed. Yet the conspiracy is dramatically necessary, as a concrete demonstration of the evil present in the play. We are

No occupation; all men idle, all;
And women too, but innocent and pure;
No sovereignty.

Sebastian.   Yet he would be king on't.

Antonio. The latter end of his commonwealth for- 160
gets the beginning.

Gonzalo. All things in common nature should produce
Without sweat or endeavor. Treason, felony,
Sword, pike, knife, gun, or need of any engine 164
Would I not have; but nature should bring forth,
Of it own kind, all foison, all abundance, 166
To feed my innocent people.

Sebastian. No marrying 'mong his subjects?

Antonio. None, man, all idle — whores and knaves.

Gonzalo. I would with such perfection govern, sir,
T' excel the golden age.

Sebastian.   Save his Majesty!

Antonio. Long live Gonzalo!

Gonzalo.   And — do you mark me, sir?

Alonso. Prithee no more. Thou dost talk nothing 173
to me.

Gonzalo. I do well believe your Highness; and did
it to minister occasion to these gentlemen, who are 176
of such sensible and nimble lungs that they always 177
use to laugh at nothing.

Antonio. 'Twas you we laughed at.

Gonzalo. Who in this kind of merry fooling am
nothing to you: so you may continue, and laugh at
nothing still.

Antonio. What a blow was there given!

Sebastian. An it had not fall'n flatlong. 184

Gonzalo. You are gentlemen of brave mettle: you
would lift the moon out of her sphere if she would 186
continue in it five weeks without changing.

Enter ARIEL, *invisible, playing solemn music.*

Sebastian. We would so, and then go a-batfowling. 188

Antonio. Nay, good my lord, be not angry.

Gonzalo. No, I warrant you: I will not adventure 190
my discretion so weakly. Will you laugh me asleep, 191
for I am very heavy?

Antonio. Go sleep, and hear us. 193

[*All sleep except* ALONSO, SEBASTIAN, *and* ANTONIO.

Alonso. What, all so soon asleep? I wish mine eyes
Would, with themselves, shut up my thoughts. I find
They are inclined to do so.

Sebastian.   Please you, sir,
Do not omit the heavy offer of it. 197
It seldom visits sorrow; when it doth,
It is a comforter.

Antonio.   We two, my lord,
Will guard your person while you take your rest,
And watch your safety.

Alonso.   Thank you. Wondrous heavy.

[ALONSO *sleeps. Exit* ARIEL.

Sebastian. What a strange drowsiness possesses
them!

160. "forgets": i.e., Gonzalo has forgotten what he has said about equality.

164. "engine": of war.

166. "it": its.
"foison": harvest, abundance.

173. "nothing to me": i.e., nothing that makes any sense to me.

176. "minister occasion": provide an opportunity.

177. "sensible and nimble": sensitive and active.

184. "An": if.
"flatlong": with the flat of the sword and not the edge.

186. "lift the moon . . .": i.e., you would take the moon out of its orbit if you could reach it.

188. "a-batfowling": (with the moon for a lantern) they would hunt birds with clubs (bats).

190. "adventure my discretion": risk my reputation.

191. "so weakly": in so minor a matter.

193. "Go sleep . . . us": compose yourself for sleep, and you will hear us laugh.

197. "omit . . . heavy offer": neglect the offer of its heaviness.

THE TEMPEST

ACT II SCENE I

sure after Act I that Ferdinand and Miranda will marry and that Prospero will regain his dukedom. Good will triumph. We need to be reminded that its triumph is not automatic. Humanity being what it is, the ship that brings the noble Ferdinand and the honest Gonzalo to the island also brings Sebastian and Antonio. Evil exists, and cannot be ignored. Ignoring it was Prospero's mistake before the play began.

Coleridge has compared the way in which Antonio insinuates the idea of murder into Sebastian's mind with Lady Macbeth's calculated preparation of her husband for the murder of Duncan: "The scene of the intended assassination of Alonzo and Gonzalo is an exact counterpart of the scene between Macbeth and his lady, only pitched in a lower key throughout, as designed to be frustrated and concealed, and exhibiting the same profound management in the manner of familiarizing a mind, not immediately recipient, to the suggestion of guilt, by associating the proposed crime with something ludicrous or out of place—something not habitually a matter of reverence."

Antonio. It is the quality o' th' climate.

Sebastian.   Why
Doth it not then our eyelids sink? I find not
Myself disposed to sleep.

Antonio.   Nor I: my spirits are nimble.
They fell together all, as by consent.
They dropped as by a thunder-stroke. What might,
Worthy Sebastian — O, what might? — No more!
And yet methinks I see it in thy face,
What thou shouldst be. Th' occasion speaks thee,
    and   210
My strong imagination sees a crown
Dropping upon thy head.

Sebastian.   What? Art thou waking? 212
Antonio. Do you not hear me speak?
Sebastian.   I do; and surely
It is a sleepy language, and thou speak'st
Out of thy sleep. What is it thou didst say?
This is a strange repose, to be asleep
With eyes wide open; standing, speaking, moving,
And yet so fast asleep.

Antonio.   Noble Sebastian,
Thou let'st thy fortune sleep — die, rather; wink'st 219
Whiles thou art waking.

Sebastian.   Thou dost snore distinctly;
There's meaning in thy snores.

Antonio. I am more serious than my custom. You 222
Must be so too, if heed me; which to do
Trebles thee o'er.

Sebastian.   Well, I am standing water. 224
Antonio. I'll teach you how to flow.
Sebastian.   Do so. To ebb
Hereditary sloth instructs me.

Antonio.   O,
If you but knew how you the purpose cherish   227
Whiles thus you mock it! how, in stripping it,   228
You more invest it! Ebbing men indeed   229
(Most often) do so near the bottom run
By their own fear or sloth.

Sebastian.   Prithee say on.
The setting of thine eye and cheek proclaim   232
A matter from thee; and a birth, indeed,   233
Which throes thee much to yield.

Antonio.   Thus, sir: 234
Although this lord of weak remembrance, this   235
Who shall be of as little memory   236
When he is earthed, hath here almost persuaded   237
(For he's a spirit of persuasion, only
Professes to persuade) the King his son's alive,
'Tis as impossible that he's undrowned
As he that sleeps here swims.

Sebastian.   I have no hope
That he's undrowned.

Antonio.   O, out of that no hope
What great hope have you! No hope that way is
Another way so high a hope that even
Ambition cannot pierce a wink beyond,   245
But doubt discovery there. Will you grant with me 246
That Ferdinand is drowned?

Sebastian.   He's gone.

210. "th' occasion speaks thee": the situation calls to you to take advantage of it.

212. "Art thou waking?": i.e., perhaps you too have fallen asleep.

219. "wink'st": sleep.

222. "than my custom": than is customary with me.

224. "trebles thee o'er": makes you three times what you are.
"standing water": i.e., as a tide, between ebbing and flowing.

227-28. "the purpose . . . it": Antonio means that Sebastian's mockery indicates that he has a spirit which will approve the traitorous plan. He is not bound by conventional reverence or respect for values.

229. "invest": clothe.
"Ebbing men": perhaps Antonio at this point makes some gesture toward the sleeping Alonso.

232. "setting": fixed expression.

233. "A matter": i.e., of importance.

234. "throes thee much": costs you much pain.

235. "weak remembrance": poor memory; Gonzalo at 154.

236. "as little memory": as little remembered.

237. "earthed": buried.

245-46. "wink": glimpse.
"Ambition cannot . . . there": the meaning of these lines is obscure; "Ambition cannot set its eye on a higher object (than the crown), and even there must have difficulty in discerning its goal" (Arden).

THE TEMPEST

ACT II SCENE I

Antonio presents the project with casual cold-bloodedness. He dismisses the difference between sleep and death, suggesting that there is no great distinction between Alonso asleep and dead— "If he were that which now he's like—that's dead." In the same way Gonzalo is only to be put to sleep—"to the perpetual wink." Neither of the victims have any importance for Antonio. (Contrast here Macbeth's agonized contemplation of Duncan's virtues.) Alonso, being unprotected, is "no better than the earth he lies upon." Gonzalo is dismissed with a sneer as "This ancient morsel, this Sir Prudence." Here we have an example of Shakespeare's ability for communicating the quality of an individual's mind through the kind of language used. Antonio's poetry is full of vivid, compressed images: "till new-born chins/ Be rough and razorable" and They'll take suggestion as a cat laps milk." The effect is of a sharp, observant mind and quick intelligence. The sense we get of Antonio's confidence and efficiency arises in part from his total lack of those promptings of morality and conscience which confuse and perturb other men. For Antonio such things are imaginative fancies, having no real existence. So when Sebastian inquires after his conscience he replies "Ay, sir, where lies that?" Does it, he asks, have the reality of a chilblain which might "put me to my slippers?" Since conscience is a "deity" which Antonio cannot "feel," it does not exist for him.

Antonio.   Then tell me,
Who's the next heir of Naples?
    Sebastian.   Claribel.
    Antonio. She that is Queen of Tunis; she that dwells
Ten leagues beyond man's life; she that from Naples   250
Can have no note, unless the sun were post —   251
The man i' th' moon's too slow — till newborn chins
Be rough and razorable; she that from whom
We all were sea-swallowed, though some cast again,   254
And, by that destiny, to perform an act
Whereof what's past is prologue, what to come,   256
Is yours and my discharge.
    Sebastian.   What stuff is this? How say you?   257
'Tis true my brother's daughter's Queen of Tunis;
So is she heir of Naples; 'twixt which regions
There is some space.
    Antonio.   A space whose ev'ry cubit
Seems to cry out "How shall that Claribel
Measure us back to Naples? Keep in Tunis,   262
And let Sebastian wake!" Say this were death,
That now hath seized them, why, they were no worse
Than now they are. There be that can rule Naples   265
As well as he that sleeps; lords that can prate
As amply and unnecessarily
As this Gonzalo; I myself could make
A chough of as deep chat. O, that you bore   269
The mind that I do! What a sleep were this
For your advancement! Do you understand me?
    Sebastian. Methinks I do.
    Antonio.   And how does your content   272
Tender your own good fortune?
    Sebastian.   I remember
You did supplant your brother Prospero.
    Antonio.   True.
And look how well my garments sit upon me,   )
Much feater than before. My brother's servants   276
Were then my fellows; now they are my men.   277
    Sebastian. But, for your conscience —
    Antonio. Ay sir, where lies that? If 'twere a kibe,   279
'Twould put me to my slipper; but I feel not   280
This deity in my bosom. Twenty consciences
That stand 'twixt me and Milan, candied be they   282
And melt, ere they molest! Here lies your brother,
No better than the earth he lies upon
If he were that which now he's like — that's dead;
Whom I with this obedient steel (three inches of it)
Can lay to bed for ever; whiles you, doing thus,
To the perpetual wink for aye might put   288
This ancient morsel, this Sir Prudence, who
Should not upbraid our course. For all the rest,
They'll take suggestion as a cat laps milk;   291
They'll tell the clock to any business that   292
We say befits the hour.
    Sebastian.   Thy case, dear friend,
Shall be my precedent. As thou got'st Milan,
I'll come by Naples. Draw thy sword. One stroke
Shall free thee from the tribute which thou payest,   296
And I the King shall love thee.
    Antonio.   Draw together;

250. "Ten leagues . . . life": i.e., it would take more than a lifetime to get there.

251. "note": communication. "post": messenger.

254. "cast": cast up.

256. "Whereof what's . . . prologue": i.e., what has happened has prepared the setting for our act.

257. "discharge": responsibility.

262. "us": the cubits. "Keep": addressed to Claribel.

265. "There be": There be those (understood).

269. "A chough . . . chat": a jackdaw talk as well, or as deeply.

272-3. "And how . . . fortune?": i.e., how do you feel about your opportunity to better yourself?

clothing imagery

276. "feater": more gracefully.

277. "fellows": equals. "men": servants.

279-280. "If 'twere . . . slipper": if it were a chilblain it would force me to wear my slipper (i.e., it is not as much trouble as a minor physical ailment).

282. "candied . . . melt": let them dissolve, like sugared candy.

288. "perpetual wink": endless sleep; death.

291. "suggestion": i.e., our suggestion, or direction.

292. "tell the clock": answer appropriately.

296. "the tribute": see I.ii.113.

question on all acts
journal entry
composition exer.
448, 459
choose 1 of 4
due Wednesday!

Antonio is the last example of a group of Shakespearean villains who appeared in the earlier plays, the most obvious representatives being Richard III, Edmund in King Lear, and Iago in Othello. They have in common a total disregard for any sort of morality or spiritual value. All their actions are prompted by a desire for power, and usually take the form of a conspiracy. In The Tempest, where the contrast between nature and society is prominent, a character such as Antonio has a further function. If Caliban represents the dangers of the natural man, then Antonio represents the dangers of the civilized man. Antonio is more evil than Caliban because he represents the inhumanity of man to man that can flourish within the framework of what is apparently a moral, civilized society.

And when I rear my hand, do you the like,
To fall it on Gonzalo.   [*They draw.*
Sebastian.   O, but one word!   299

Enter ARIEL, *invisible, with music and song.*

Ariel. My master through his art forsees the danger
That you, his friend, are in, and sends me forth   301
(For else his project dies) to keep them living.   302

[*Sings in* GONZALO's *ear.*

While you here do snoring lie,
Open-eyed conspiracy   304
    His time doth take.
If of life you keep a care,
Shake off slumber and beware.
    Awake, awake!

Antonio. Then let us both be sudden.
Gonzalo. [*wakes*]   Now good angels 309
Preserve the King!
Alonso. Why, how now? — Ho, awake! — Why are you drawn?   311
Wherefore this ghastly looking?
Gonzalo.   What's the matter?
Sebastian. Whiles we stood here securing your repose,   313
Even now, we heard a hollow burst of bellowing
Like bulls, or rather lions. Did't not wake you?
It struck mine ear most terribly.
Alonso.   I heard nothing.
Antonio. O, 'twas a din to fright a monster's ear,
To make an earthquake! Sure it was the roar
Of a whole herd of lions.
Alonso.   Heard you this, Gonzalo?
Gonzalo. Upon mine honor, sir, I heard a humming, 320
And that a strange one too, which did awake me.
I shaked you sir, and cried. As mine eyes opened,
I saw their weapons drawn. There was a noise,
That's verily. 'Tis best we stand upon our guard,
Or that we quit this place. Let's draw our weapons.
Alonso. Lead off this ground, and let's make further search
For my poor son.
Gonzalo.   Heavens keep him from these beasts!
For he is sure i' th' island.
Alonso.   Lead away.
Ariel. Prospero my lord shall know what I have done.
So, King, go safely on to seek thy son.   [*Exeunt.*

299. "but one word!": one word more.

301-02. "That you . . . living": Ariel speaks first to Gonzalo ("you") and then to the audience ("to keep them living").

304. "Open-eyed": in contrast to the sleeping Gonzalo.

309. "sudden": quick.

311. "drawn": with swords drawn.

313. "securing": watching over, guarding.

320. "a humming": Ariel's song.

Caliban enters, cursing Prospero, although he knows that punishment must follow. We know enough of Caliban already to see him as the irredeemable animal element in man. Regarded symbolically, his confinement by Prospero and his frequent disciplining through punishment represent the constant control and direction that man-as-spirit (represented by Prospero) must exercise over man-as-animal. However Caliban is also a character in the play, and it is interesting to notice two points concerning him in this scene: (1) he speaks poetry, whereas Stephano and Trinculo speak prose and (2) he is constantly aware of the spirits of the island. Stephano and Trinculo are not, except when Ariel intends them to be. These points are related. They both indicate a certain natural sensitivity on Caliban's part (he is given some of the most lyrical poetry in the play) which the Neapolitan city dwellers lack. This is an aspect of the paradox of Caliban's character: on the one hand he represents instinctive, sometimes brutal, nature (as in the attempted rape of Miranda). On the other hand his intimacy with the natural world gives him a quality of sensitivity which they lack. He is punished by the spirits as apes, hedgehogs and adders because he is himself an animal. His poetry everywhere suggests his complete identity with and understanding of the natural world around him.

Trinculo, who now appears, is described in the Dramatis Personae as a "jester," which probably means he wears the "pied" or multi-colored costume of the court clown. He is not a comic in the sense of making jokes. He is the foil for Stephano and Caliban in the comic interludes. He follows them, hesitant and timorous, and both of them bully him to some extent. One director has said that "with the possible exception of Malvolio, Trinculo is the most neurotic of Shakespeare's comic characters. His stage life is a progress from fear to fear, beginning with the weather. His mind is more sensitive than Stephano's, but its only introductions are to terror and misery."

Scene two.

(ANOTHER PART OF THE ISLAND)

Enter CALIBAN *with a burden of wood. A noise of thunder heard.*

Caliban. All the infections that the sun sucks up
From bogs, fens, flats, on Prosper fall, and make him
By inchmeal a disease! His spirits hear me,   3
And yet I needs must curse. But they'll nor pinch,
Fright me with urchin-shows, pitch me i' th' mire,   5
Nor lead me, like a firebrand, in the dark   6
Out of my way, unless he bid 'em; but
For every trifle are they set upon me;   8
Sometime like apes that mow and chatter at me,   9
And after bite me; then like hedgehogs which
Lie tumbling in my barefoot way and mount
Their pricks at my footfall; sometime am I
All wound with adders, who with cloven tongues   13
Do hiss me into madness.

Enter TRINCULO.

       Lo, now, lo!
Here comes a spirit of his, and to torment me
For bringing wood in slowly. I'll fall flat.
Perchance he will not mind me.   [*Lies down.*

Trinculo. Here's neither bush nor shrub to bear off   18
any weather at all, and another storm brewing: I
hear it sing i' th' wind. Yond same black cloud, yond
huge one, looks like a foul bombard that would shed   21
his liquor. If it should thunder as it did before, I
know not where to hide my head. Yond same cloud
cannot choose but fall by pailfuls. What have we
here? a man or a fish? dead or alive? A fish: he
smells like a fish; a very ancient and fishlike smell;
a kind of not of the newest poor-John. A strange fish!   27
Were I in England now, as once I was, and had but
this fish painted, not a holiday fool there but would   29
give a piece of silver. There would this monster
make a man: any strange beast there makes a man   31
When they will not give a doit to relieve a lame beg-   32
gar, they will lay out ten to see a dead Indian.
Legged like a man! and his fins like arms! Warm, o'   34
my troth! I do now let loose my opinion, hold it no
longer: this is no fish, but an islander, that hath
lately suffered by a thunderbolt. [*Thunder.*] Alas,
the storm is come again! My best way is to creep
under his gaberdine: there is no other shelter here-   39
about. Misery acquaints a man with strange bed-
fellows. I will here shroud till the dregs of the storm
be past.   [*Creeps under* CALIBAN's *garment.*

Enter STEPHANO, *singing; a bottle in his hand.*

Stephano.   I shall no more to sea, to sea;
       Here shall I die ashore.
This is a very scurvy tune to sing at a man's funeral.
Well, here's my comfort.   [*Drinks.*

3. "By inchmeal": inch by inch.

5. "urchin-shows": it was an Elizabethan folk belief that malignant spirits appeared in the form of hedgehogs to torment people.

6. "like a firebrand": in the form of a will-o'-the-wisp.

8. "every trifle": the smallest reason.

9. "mow": make faces.

13. "All wound": twined about with.

17. "mind": pay attention to.

18. "bear off": protect from.

21. "bombard": leather bottle.

27. "poor-John": dried hake, a fish related to cod.

29. "painted": painted on a sign outside a booth at a fair.

31. "make": make money for.

32. "doit": small coin.

34. "Legged like a man!": Caliban is represented in many forms on the stage. "Caliban's dress is a large bear skin, or the skin of some other animal; and he is usually represented with long shaggy hair" (Malone). "Although he is occasionally called a fish this is largely because of his oddity, and there should be no fishiness about his appearance" (Arden edition).

39. "gaberdine": cloak.

THE TEMPEST

ACT II, SCENE II

Stephano and Trinculo speak prose and the scenes in which they appear are, by and large, prose scenes. Shakespeare uses prose for various reasons: (1) rhythms of blank verse, continued overlong, become monotonous to the ear; (2) prose provides a rhythmic change of pace for the audience. In Shakespearean comedy, prose used is usually to distinguish the low characters from the heroes, heroines and more socially exalted figures, who speak poetry, as in The Tempest. This is not to say that there is any imaginative decline in the language when prose replaces verse. Shakespeare's prose has its own special, vivid power.

Trinculo's first reaction to the figure of Caliban is significant: he reflects on the money he might make out of him. Shakespeare makes him single out England as a special exemplification of the gullibility and selfishness of the crowd: "When they will not give a doit to relieve a lame beggar, they will lay out ten to see a dead Indian." Stephano, when he arrives, reacts in just the same way to Caliban. He will be a source of profit "if I can recover him, and keep him tame, and get to Naples with him." Caliban may be, as Prospero says, a "thing of darkness," but the two Neapolitans represent the manner in which social man may also be corrupt and debased.

While Stephano is described as a "butler" he is obviously a sea-going butler, or sailor-turned-butler, as we see from his bawdy sailor's drinking song and subsequent nautical references. Shakespeare may have made him the ship's butler to account for his access to the cask of wine on which he floated ashore (although at one point he maintains that he swam "five-and-thirty leagues off and on"). The Dramatis Personae also describes Stephano as "drunken," and he is so throughout the play, with some possible sobering at the end, under Prospero's punishment.

The master, the swabber, the boatswain, and I, 47
    The gunner, and his mate,
Loved Mall, Meg, and Marian, and Margery,
    But none of us cared for Kate.
    For she had a tongue with a tang,
    Would cry to a sailor "Go hang!"
She loved not the savor of tar nor of pitch; 53
Yet a tailor might scratch her wher'er she did 54
    itch.
    Then to sea, boys, and let her go hang!

This is a scurvy tune too; but here's my comfort. [*Drinks.*

Caliban. Do not torment me! O!

Stephano. What's the matter? Have we devils here? Do you put tricks upon 's with savages and men of Inde, ha? I have not scaped drowning to be afeard now of your four legs; for it hath been said, "As proper a man as ever went on four legs cannot 62 make him give ground"; and it shall be said so again, while Stephano breathes at nostrils.

Caliban. The spirit torments me. O!

Stephano. This is some monster of the isle, with four legs, who hath got, as I take it, an ague. Where 67 the devil should he learn our language? I will give him some relief, if it be but for that. If I can recover him, and keep him tame, and get to Naples with him, he's a present for any emperor that ever trod on neat's leather. 72

Caliban. Do not torment me, prithee; I'll bring my wood home faster.

Stephano. He's in his fit now and does not talk after the wisest. He shall taste of my bottle: if he have never drunk wine afore, it will go near to remove his fit. If I can recover him and keep him tame, I will not take too much for him; he shall pay 79 for him that hath him, and that soundly.

Caliban. Thou dost me yet but little hurt.
Thou wilt anon; I know it by thy trembling.
Now Prosper works upon thee.

Stephano. Come on your ways: open your mouth: here is that which will give language to you, cat. 85 Open your mouth. This will shake your shaking, I can tell you, and that soundly. [*Gives* CALIBAN *drink.*] You cannot tell who's your friend. Open your chaps again. 89

Trinculo. I should know that voice. It should be — but he is drowned; and these are devils. O, defend me!

Stephano. Four legs and two voices — a most delicate monster! His forward voice now is to speak well of his friend; his backward voice is to utter foul speeches and to detract. If all the wine in my bottle will recover him, I will help his ague. Come! [*Gives drink*]. Amen! I will pour some in thy other mouth.

Trinculo. Stephano!

Stephano. Doth thy other mouth call me? Mercy, mercy! This is a devil, and no monster. I will leave him; I have no long spoon. 103

47. "The master . . .": Stephano's song was presumably accompanied by music offstage.

53. "tar . . . pitch": associated with sailors.

54. "a tailor": members of this trade were, for some reason, the butt of many indecent jokes in Elizabethan plays.

62. "four legs": Stephano's confused modification of the proverb 'As proper a man as ever went on two legs . . .'

67. "ague": fever.

72. "neat's leather": cowhide.

79. "too much": i.e., all I can get.

85. "cat": reference to the proverb "Liquor will make a cat talk."

89. "chaps": jaws.

103. "long spoon": reference to the proverb "He who sups with the devil must have a long spoon."

THE TEMPEST

ACT II, SCENE II

According to one set of standards he is a bully, a coward, a boaster and a fool. He is also one of Shakespeare's most memorable comic creations and in a world which contains Sebastian and Antonio, it is difficult to disapprove of him. If we see the play as dramatizing various human qualities, then Stephano represents all that is coarse, unimaginative and durable in ordinary, unheroic humanity. Like Bottom and Falstaff he is absolutely sure of himself, indeed convinced of his superiority to those about him. "We will inherit here," he says, looking confidently about the island, and takes his acclamation as "King Stephano" (IV.i) as only right and natural. The comedy lies in the fact that he has not the faintest notion of his real position as he staggers about the island, plotting Prospero's overthrow, waving his bottle, and haranguing his two subjects.

We have already seen the way in which Caliban's "You taught me language, and my profit on't/ Is, I know how to curse" can be interpreted as a sharp comment on the civilizing process that a higher culture can inflict upon a native, or lower culture. The relation between Stephano and Caliban makes the same comment in a more elaborate form. When Stephano reels onstage Caliban's first recation is "That's a brave god and bears celestial liquor./ I will kneel to him." For the rest of the scene Stephano plies Caliban with his bottle of sack, and as the latter's consciousness deteriorates, his reverence grows: "I will kiss thy foot. I prithee be my god." Here the civilizing influence of society is represented by the drink, which produces in Caliban the illusion that he has found a kind of freedom, and has escaped the domination of Prospero at last — the natural man, freed by drink, casts off the control of the rational man. This illusion leads him, finally, into the horse pond, and stern punishment from Prospero. (When we recall some of the damaging side-effects of the white man's civiliza-

Trinculo. Stephano! If thou beest Stephano, touch me and speak to me; for I am Trinculo — be not afeard — thy good friend Trinculo.

Stephano. If thou beest Trinculo, come forth. I'll pull thee by the lesser legs. If any be Trinculo's legs, these are they.

[Draws him out from under CALIBAN'S *garment.]*

Thou art very Trinculo indeed: how cam'st thou to be the siege of this mooncalf? Can he vent 111 Trinculos?

Trinculo. I took him to be killed with a thunderstroke. But art thou not drowned, Stephano? I hope now thou art not drowned. Is the storm overblown? I hid me under the dead mooncalf's gaberdine for fear of the storm. And art thou living, Stephano? O Stephano, two Neapolitans scaped!

Stephano. Prithee do not turn me about: my stomach is not constant.

Caliban. [*aside*] These be fine things, an if they be
    not sprites.   121
That's a brave god and bears celestial liquor.
I will kneel to him.

Stephano. How didst thou scape? How cam'st thou hither? Swear by this bottle how thou cam'st hither. I escaped upon a butt of sack which the sailors heaved o'erboard, by this bottle, which I made of the bark of a tree with mine own hands since I was cast ashore.

Caliban. I'll swear upon that bottle to be thy true subject, for the liquor is not earthly.

Stephano. Here! Swear then how thou escapedst.

Trinculo. Swum ashore, man, like a duck. I can swim like a duck, I'll be sworn.

Stephano. Here, kiss the book. [*Gives him drink.*] 135 Though thou canst swim like a duck, thou art made like a goose.

Trinculo. O Stephano, hast any more of this?

Stephano. The whole butt, man: my cellar is in a rock by th' seaside, where my wine is hid. How now, mooncalf? How does thine ague?

Caliban. Hast thou not dropped from heaven?

Stephano. Out o' th' moon, I do assure thee. I was the Man i' th' Moon when time was.   144

Caliban. I have seen thee in her, and I do adore
    thee.
My mistress showed me thee, and thy dog, and thy
    bush.

Stephano. Come, swear to that; kiss the book. I will furnish it anon with new contents. Swear.

                                                [Caliban drinks.

Trinculo. By this good light, this is a very shallow monster! I afeard of him? A very weak monster! The Man i' th' Moon? A most poor credulous monster!—Well drawn, monster, in good sooth!   152

Caliban. I'll show thee every fertile inch o' th' island;
And I will kiss thy foot. I prithee be my god.

Trinculo. By this light, a most perfidious and drunken monster! When god's asleep, he'll rob his bottle.

---

111. "siege": excretion.
    "mooncalf": monstrosity.

121. "an if": if.

135. "kiss the book": i.e., the bottle; Caliban regards Stephano as a god, and the performance is a parody of a religious ceremony, with the bottle as a sacred book.

144. "when time was": once upon a time.

152. "Well drawn": a good draught (of wine).

ACT II, SCENE II

tion on native populations in the New World, Shakespeare's foresight seems uncanny.) A second comic element in the exchanges between Stephano and Caliban may also be relevant to the effect of the European colonizer on the native. Caliban affirms, in the first glow of discovery, that Stephano's "liquor is not earthly." A few lines later he asks Stephano whether he has not "dropped from Heaven." He sees Stephano as a god, and the liquor provides a kind of mystical, religious experience. Stephano's language underlines this idea. "Kiss the book" is the way he commands Caliban to drink from his bottle. The members of the Elizabethan audience, more aware than we are of the ritual reverence done to the scriptures, would certainly see this as a parody of the worshiper kissing the bible. Caliban is not only a willing slave of the new "god" Stephano, he is also a convert to a new religion, whose "book" imparts novel sensations of self-confidence and belief. The whole scene is a wonderful parody of (1) the way in which the apparently 'civilized' man may appear to have a magical value to the uncivilized and (2) the sort of primitive religious conversion which resembles intoxication in its irrational emotionalism. It is Trinculo who, standing aside, provides the explanatory comment on Caliban's behavior: "A most ridiculous monster, to make a wonder of a poor drunkard!" At the scene's end Caliban staggers offstage after his new god and leader with shouts of "Freedom, high-day!" having exchanged a known bondage for a new and unknown one.

ACT III, SCENE I

The stage direction opening the scene — "Enter Ferdinand, bearing a log"—is a significant repetition of the opening stage direction of the preceding scene—"Enter Caliban with a burden of wood." Both are serving Prospero in menial labor. The contrast in what they say is also significant. Caliban "needs must curse." It is his nature to rebel, and in fact he ends by guiding a conspiracy against Prospero. Caliban as a natural, instinctive being resents direction, and cannot submit to bondage since he is un-

Caliban. I'll kiss thy foot. I'll swear myself thy
    subject.
Stephano. Come on then. Down, and swear!
Trinculo. I shall laugh myself to death at this puppy-headed monster. A most scurvy monster! I could find in my heart to beat him —
Stephano. Come, kiss.
Trinculo. But that the poor monster's in drink. An abominable monster!
Caliban. I'll show thee the best springs; I'll pluck
    thee berries;
I'll fish for thee, and get thee wood enough.
A plague upon the tyrant that I serve!
I'll bear him no more sticks, but follow thee,
Thou wondrous man.
Trinculo. A most ridiculous monster, to make a wonder of a poor drunkard!
Caliban. I prithee let me bring thee where crabs 173
    grow;
And I with my long nails will dig thee pignuts, 174
Show thee a jay's nest, and instruct thee how
To snare the nimble marmoset; I'll bring thee 176
To clust'ring filberts, and sometimes I'll get thee
Young scamels from the rock. Wilt thou go with me? 178
  Stephano. I prithee now, lead the way without any more talking. Trinculo, the King and all our company else being drowned, we will inherit here. Here, 181
bear my bottle. Fellow Trinculo, we'll fill him by and by again. | CALIBAN *sings drunkenly.*
Caliban. Farewell, master; farewell, farewell!
Trinculo. A howling monster! a drunken monster!
Caliban. No more dams I'll make for fish.
    No fetch in firing 187
      At requiring,
    Nor scrape trenchers, nor wash dish. 189
    'Ban, 'Ban, Ca—Caliban 190
    Has a new master: get a new man.
Freedom, high-day! high-day, freedom! freedom, high-day, freedom!
  Stephano. O brave monster! lead the way. [*Exeunt.*

173. "crabs": crabapples.

174. "pignuts": peanuts.

176. "marmoset": a small monkey.

178. "scamels": this term has never been satisfactorily explained, but is probably a misprint for sea-mell or sea-mew, a rock-nesting bird.

181. "we will inherit": we take complete possession.

187. "firing": firewood.

189. "trenchers nor wash dish": onions nor wash plates.

190. "Ca-Caliban": suggests drunkenness, and the way in which the actor should play the end of the scene.

ACT THREE, scene one.

(BEFORE PROSPERO'S CELL)

Enter FERDINAND, *bearing a log.*

Ferdinand. There be some sports are painful, and
    their labor 1
Delight in them sets off; some kinds of baseness
Are nobly undergone, and most poor matters 3
Point to rich ends. This my mean task
Would be as heavy to me as odious, but
The mistress which I serve quickens what's dead 6
And makes my labors pleasures. O, she is
Ten times more gentle than her father's crabbed;
And he's composed of harshness! I must remove 9
Some thousands of these logs and pile them up,

1. "painful": difficult.
"labor . . . off": i.e., their difficulty makes their pleasure greater by contrast.

3. "most poor . . . ends": i.e., lowly duties lead to great results.

6. "quickens": brings to life.

9. "composed": made of nothing but.

THE TEMPEST

ACT III, SCENE I

[handwritten note:] Caliban + Ferdinand
servants of Prospero
Caliban does not
see necessity of
servitude
Ferdinand does

able to understand that it may be necessary in order to achieve something else. Ferdinand takes the opposite position. He has both pride and nobility, as his first attempts to oppose Prospero demonstrated. However his love for Miranda makes him see that bondage, submission and sacrifice are necessary to win her. He is taught, as Caliban could not be, that the natural, instinctive resentment of control is wrong and must be overcome if any final value is to be achieved.

The idea of sacrifice or deprivation as a necessary preliminary to some higher fulfilment runs through the play. Like Caliban and Ferdinand, Ariel is also serving a term of bondage, about which he complains, until Prospero explains sharply to him that this is the price of his freedom. Prospero himself had to endure the bondage of being an island castaway, before emerging as the master of all the other destinies in the play. This accounts for his harshness to Ariel and Miranda, both of whom he loves. He understands the purgatorial necessity of hardship and discipline as they do not.

Upon a sore injunction. My sweet mistress 11
Weeps when she sees me work, and says such
   baseness 12
Had never like executor. I forget;
But these sweet thoughts do even refresh my labors
Most busy least, when I do it.

Enter MIRANDA; *and* PROSPERO *behind, unseen.*

Miranda.   Alas, now pray you 15
Work not so hard! I would the lightning had
Burnt up those logs that you are enjoined to pile!
Pray set it down and rest you. When this burns,
Some thousands of these logs and pile them up,
'Twill weep for having wearied you. My father 19
Is hard at study: pray now rest yourself.
He's safe for these three hours.
Ferdinand.   O most dear mistress,
The sun will set before I shall discharge
What I must strive to do.
Miranda.   If you'll sit down,
I'll bear your logs the while. Pray give me that:
I'll carry it to the pile.
Ferdinand.   No, precious creature:
I had rather crack my sinews, break my back,
Than you should such dishonor undergo
While I sit lazy by.
Miranda.   It would become me 28
As well as it does you; and I should do it
With much more ease; for my good will is to it,
And yours it is against.
Prospero. [*aside*] Poor worm, thou art infected
This visitation shows it.
Miranda.   You look wearily. 32
Ferdinand. No, noble mistress: 'tis fresh morning
   with me 33
When you are by at night. I do beseech you, 34
Chiefly that I might set it in my prayers,
What is your name?
Miranda.   Miranda. O my father,
I have broke your hest to say so!
Ferdinand.   Admired Miranda! 37
Indeed the top of admiration, worth 38
What's dearest to the world! Full many a lady
I have eyed with best regard, and many a time 40
Th' harmony of their tongues hath into bondage
Brought my too diligent ear; for several virtues 42
Have I liked several women; never any 43
With so full soul but some defect in her 44
Did quarrel with the noblest grace she owed,
And put it to the foil. But you, O you, 46
So perfect and so peerless, are created
Of every creature's best.
Miranda.   I do not know
One of my sex; no woman's face remember, 49
Save, from my glass, mine own; nor have I seen
More that I may call men than you, good friend,
And my dear father. How features are abroad 52
I am skilless of; but, by my modesty

11. "sore injunction": stern command.

12. "such baseness . . . executor": such a lowly task was never done by one so noble.

15. "Most busy . . . it": i.e., when I am busy, I am least conscious of being busy (because of the "sweet thoughts").

19. " 'Twill weep": Miranda's fanciful term refers to water or resin oozing from the burning wood.

28. "become": suit.

32. "visitation": to Ferdinand.

33-4. "fresh . . . night": the familiar Elizabethan notion of the lady (like the sun) turning night into day.

37. "hest": command.

38. "admiration": wonder (see I.ii.427).

40. "best regard": highest approval.

42. "diligent": closely-attending.

43. "several": various.

44. "With so full soul": so completely.

46. "put . . . foil": set it off by contrast.

49. "remember": it has been objected that Miranda did remember her waiting women (I.ii.46) but such details are unimportant in a dramatic presentation, and Shakespeare is frequently careless of them.

52. "abroad": elsewhere in the world.

The declarations of love between Ferdinand and Miranda are expressed in poetry of a highly formal, almost impersonal kind. This is not meant to be a naturalistic or realistic love scene. When Shakespeare wanted to show love as a powerful passion, which might oscillate between rapture and anger, he was able to do so, as we can see in Othello and Antony and Cleopatra. Here the intention is different. The love between Ferdinand and Miranda is part of the play's larger pattern. The purity and innocence of their love in its simple affirmation atones for the suspicions, hostilities and betrayals of their fathers' generation. The pattern recurs in several of Shakespeare's last plays. The sins of the fathers are visited on, but also atoned for by the children.

(The jewel in my dower), I would not wish
Any companion in the world but you;
Nor can imagination form a shape,
Besides yourself, to like of. But I prattle
Something too wildly, and my father's precepts
I therein do forget.
    Ferdinand.   I am, in my condition,   59
A prince, Miranda; I do think, a king
(I would not so), and would no more endure
This wooden slavery than to suffer
The flesh fly blow my mouth. Hear my soul speak!   63
The very instant that I saw you, did
My heart fly to your service; there resides,
To make me slave to it; and for your sake
Am I this patient log-man.
    Miranda.   Do you love me?
    Ferdinand. O heaven, O earth, bear witness to this sound,
And crown what I profess with kind event   69
If I speak true! if hollowly, invert
What best is boded me to mischief! I,   71
Beyond all limit of what else i' th' world,
Do love, prize, honor you.
    Miranda.   I am a fool
To weep at what I am glad of.
    Prospero.   [*aside*] Fair encounter
Of two most rare affections! Heavens rain grace
On that which breeds between 'em!
    Ferdinand.   Wherefore weep you?
    Miranda. At mine unworthiness, that dare not offer
What I desire to give, and much less take
What I shall die to want. But this is trifling;   79
And all the more it seeks to hide itself,
The bigger bulk it shows. Hence, bashful cunning,   81
And prompt me, plain and holy innocence!
I am your wife, if you will marry me;
If not, I'll die your maid. To be your fellow   84
You may deny me; but I'll be your servant,
Whether you will or no.
    Ferdinand.   My mistress, dearest,
And I thus humble ever.
    Miranda.   My husband then?   87
    Ferdinand. Ay, with a heart as willing
As bondage e'er of freedom. Here's my hand.   89
    Miranda. And mine, with my heart in't; and now farewell
Till half an hour hence.
    Ferdinand.   A thousand thousand!

      [*Exeunt* FERDINAND *and* MIRANDA *severally.*

    Prospero. So glad of this as they I cannot be,
Who are surprised withal; but my rejoicing   93
At nothing can be more. I'll to my book;
For yet ere supper time must I perform
Much business appertaining.   [*Exit.*   96

59. "condition": in my proper situation.

63. "blow": befoul.

69. "kind event": favorable result.

71. "is boded": is in store for.

79. "want": lack.

81. "bashful cunning": coyness.

84. "maid": in the senses of (1) virgin, (2) servant (as in 85). "fellow": equal.

87. "thus humble": Ferdinand kneels at this point.

89. "of freedom": i.e., to win freedom.

93. "Who are surprised": i.e., Ferdinand and Miranda, who were unaware of what was to happen to them.

96. "appertaining": pertaining to this new development.

Sometimes acts like chorus

Trinculo behaves in an erratic and confused way, but he is sometimes given lines which have a sort of choric value. They sum up and explain for the audience, as the chorus did in classical drama, the position of the characters and the general state of the action. We have heard one such line already—"A most ridiculous monster, to make a wonder of a poor drunkard!" There is another at the opening of this scene: "They say there's but five of us upon this isle: we are three of them. If th' other two be brained like us, the state totters." Caliban's tongue is "drowned in sack." Stephano has by now only the most confused idea of what he is doing and on what mission he is proceeding. Drunkenness has. from time immemorial, been a staple of stage comedy. The drunken person represents, in the simplest form, the situation which makes us laugh: the sight of someone doing what he is perfectly sure is sensible (the vaudeville drunk who tips his hat politely to the lamppost) when we know it is nonsense. The comedy of a comic figure arises from his misconception of his situation: the drunk can always be depended upon to misconstrue what is going on around him. In this scene much of the drunken comedy is visual, and must be brought out by the actors, as they gyrate wildly about the stage. In reading, we must supply this element from our imagination.

Scene two.

(ANOTHER PART OF THE ISLAND)

Enter CALIBAN, STEPHANO, *and* TRINCULO.

Stephano. Tell not me! When the butt is out, we will drink water; not a drop before. Therefore bear up and board 'em! Servant monster, drink to me.   1   2

Trinculo. Servant monster? The folly of this island! They say there's but five upon this isle: we are three of them. If th' other two be brained like us, the state totters.   4   6

Stephano. Drink, servant monster, when I bid thee: thy eyes are almost set in thy head.   9

Trinculo. Where should they be set else? He were a brave monster indeed if they were set in his tail.

Stephano. My man-monster hath drowned his tongue in sack. For my part, the sea cannot drown me. I swam, ere I could recover the shore, five-and-thirty leagues off and on, by this light. Thou shalt be my lieutenant, monster, or my standard.   14   16

Trinculo. Your lieutenant, if you list; he's no standard.   18

Stephano. We'll not run, Monsieur Monster.   19

Trinculo. Nor go neither; but you'll lie like dogs, and yet say nothing neither.   20

Stephano. Mooncalf, speak once in thy life, if thou beest a good mooncalf.

Caliban. How does thy honor? Let me lick thy shoe.
I'll not serve him; he is not valiant.   25

Trinculo. Thou liest, most ignorant monster: I am in case to justle a constable. Why, thou deboshed fish thou, was there ever man a coward that hath drunk so much sack as I today? Wilt thou tell a monstrous lie, being but half a fish and half a monster?   27

Caliban. Lo, how he mocks me! Wilt thou let him, my lord?

Trinculo. "Lord" quoth he? That a monster should be such a natural!   35

Caliban. Lo, lo, again! Bite him to death, I prithee.   36

Stephano. Trinculo, keep a good tongue in your head. If you prove a mutineer — the next tree! The poor monster's my subject, and he shall not suffer indignity.   37

Caliban. I thank my noble lord. Wilt thou be pleased
To hearken once again to the suit I made to thee?

Stephano. Marry, will I. Kneel and repeat it; I will stand, and so shall Trinculo.

Enter ARIEL, *invisible.*

Caliban. As I told thee before, I am subject to a tyrant,
A sorcerer, that by his cunning hath
Cheated me of the island.

Ariel. Thou liest.

Caliban.   Thou liest, thou jesting monkey thou!

1. "out": empty.
2. "bear up . . . 'em": a nautical variation of drink up.
4. "the folly": the freak, i.e. Caliban.
6. "be brained": in two senses, (1) have brains like ours, (2) as we have been brained, beaten over the head (by the wine) as we have been. The second meaning is ironic, understood by the audience but not by Trinculo or his listeners.
9. "almost set": almost disappeared, as in a sunset. In the next line Trinculo takes the word in the sense of 'placed'.
14. "recover": reach.
16. "standard": standard bearer, ensign.
18. "no standard": punning on Stephano's use of the word: Caliban can hardly stand by this time.
19. "We'll not run": i.e., from the enemy; both are staggering heavily at this point.
20. "go": walk.
25. "him": Trinculo.
27. "in case to": in a condition to. "justle": jostle, interfere with. "deboshed": debauched.
35. "natural": a fool; Trinculo means that although a monster is by definition unnatural, this one is a natural as well.
36. "again!": i.e., he has mocked me again.
37. "good tongue": as in, keep a civil tongue in your head.

Stephano's talk of Caliban as his "lieutenant" indicates that Stephano believes himself to be ruling over his court—he has "inherited here," and the other two are his soldiers and subjects. Trinculo is told that he will hang from the next tree if he "proves a mutineer," and Caliban must kneel to make his petitions. Stephano is a stern commander. This burlesque of kingship and sovereignty is richly comic, but it is more than just that. Earlier in the play we have seen evidence of disunity and strife in the social order. Here disunity takes the form of the rivalry between Trinculo and Caliban inflamed by Ariel's imitation of Trinculo's voice. The three characters are reduced to total confusion, with Stephano trying to dispense a wild and woolly kind of justice. In his earlier comedies Shakespeare frequently used the plot device of making a play's subplot (usually concerning low characters) reflect the actions of main plot (the chief characters) in such a way that the first became a parody of the second. Something of this sort happens here. The absurdity of the Trinculo-Caliban rivalry, and the officious stupidity with which Stephano plays the role of sovereign suggest that in the whole of society, from the King of Naples down to his drunken butler, such struggles for power and authority have something both childish and illusory about them. There is also a reflection on the intrigue of Sebastian and Antonio since there, as well as here, the actions of the human beings are, without their knowing it, controlled and directed by a supernatural power, taking the form of Ariel in both cases. Again, the plot to overthrow Prospero, according to which Stephano and Miranda will be king and queen, while Caliban and Trinculo become viceroys makes a further implicit comment on the stupidity of man's desire for power. In the subplot this stupidity is obvious. But the suggestion is that in the intrigue of the main plot, the goal is just as illusory despite Antonio's worldliness and cunning.

I would my valiant master would destroy thee. I do
 not lie.
 Stephano. Trinculo, if you trouble him any more
in's tale, by this hand, I will supplant some of your 51
teeth.
 Trinculo. Why, I said nothing.
 Stephano. Mum then, and no more. — Proceed.
 Caliban. I say by sorcery he got this isle;
From me he got it. If thy greatness will
Revenge it on him — for I know thou dar'st,
But this thing dare not — 58
 Stephano. That's most certain.
 Caliban. Thou shalt be lord of it, and I'll serve
 thee.
 Stephano. How now shall this be compassed?
Canst thou bring me to the party? 62
 Caliban. Yea, yea, my lord! I'll yield him thee
 asleep,
Where thou mayst knock a nail into his head.
 Ariel. Thou liest; thou canst not.
 Caliban. What a pied ninny's this! Thou scurvy 66
 patch!
I do beseech thy greatness give him blows
And take his bottle from him. When that's gone,
He shall drink naught but brine, for I'll not show
 him
Where the quick freshes are. 70
 Stephano. Trinculo, run into no further danger:
interrupt the monster one word further and, by this
hand, I'll turn my mercy out o' doors and make a
stockfish of thee. 74
 Trinculo. Why, what did I? I did nothing. I'll go
farther off.
 Stephano. Didst thou not say he lied?
 Ariel. Thou liest.
 Stephano. Do I so? Take thou that! [*Strikes Trinculo.*] As you like this, give me the lie another time. 80
 Trinculo. I did not give the lie. Out o' your wits,
and hearing too? A pox o' your bottle! This can
sack and drinking do. A murrain on your monster, 83
and the devil take your fingers!
 Caliban. Ha, ha, ha!
 Stephano. Now forward with your tale.—Prithee 86
stand further off. 87
 Caliban. Beat him enough. After a little time
I'll beat him too.
 Stephano.   Stand farther. — Come, proceed.
 Caliban. Why, as I told thee, 'tis a custom with him
I' th' afternoon to sleep: there thou mayst brain him,
Having first seized his books, or with a log
Batter his skull, or paunch him with a stake, 93
Or cut his wesand with thy knife. Remember 94
First to possess his books; for without them
He's but a sot, as I am, nor hath not 96
One spirit to command. They all do hate him
As rootedly as I. Burn but his books.
He has brave utensils (for so he calls them) 99
Which, when he has a house, he'll deck withal.
And that most deeply to consider is
The beauty of his daughter. He himself
Calls her a nonpariel. I never saw a woman 103

51. "supplant": uproot, displace.

58. "this thing": Trinculo.

62. "party": person.

66. "pied ninny": a fool; "pied" refers to the multi-colored jester's costume worn by Trinculo.
"patch": clown, from the patched dress.

70. "quick freshes": fresh-water springs.

74. "stockfish": dried fish, which was prepared by beating.

80. "give me the lie": tell me I lie.

83. "murrain": a disease of cattle.

86-87. "Prithee stand further off": this may be played in two ways, a) Stephano motions Trinculo away, or b) Caliban approaches Stephano, who cannot stand his smell.

93. "paunch": stab.

94. "wesand": windpipe.

96. "sot": here a fool, rather than a drunkard.

99. "utensils": furnishings.

103. "nonpareil": without equal.

so I can't believe Caliban would be completely serious.

94. Trinculo becomes very afraid and begins to feel bad about all the sins he repents. Stephano repents, but is not quite as afraid as Trinculo.

95. Caliban sees his work as slavery and despises every second of it. ~~Caliban~~ Ariel sees his work as price for freedom, and therefore does not mind it all that much.

96. Alonso repents because he is not as bad as the other, and has the ability to repent, while the others are too bad to be able to repent.

Carrie Hudspeth   October 17, 1995
                  Tempest Questions - Act 3

82. This sililoquoy by Ferdinand shows us that
Ferdinand does not mind being in servitude as
long as he was near Miranda and he loves her.

83. Prospero means Ferdinand is in love and that
this visit of watching them proves it.

85. Miranda omits Caliban because he is not fully
human, but part beast, so she does not feel she
can compare herself to him.

86. Prospero loves the idea of Ferdinand and Miranda
falling in love.

87. Prospero is not suprised that they have fallen
in love and pledged to marry each other because
he could see it in their eyes and expected to
happen sooner or later. He rejoices because
they do not have all the hostilities, betrayals, and
suspicions of his generations.

90
88. This is a parodie of the first plot because although
they mean it sericusly, the readers know it will
never really happen.

91. I would characterize Caliban's suggestions
as a combination of both. Although I do not
doubt that he hates Prospero, but the thought
that he would actually kill him is harder.
Also, the whole play is in a humorous fashion,

We have another example in this scene of the double nature of Caliban (see commentary at I.ii). On the one hand he is the natural being at its lowest and coarsest, "a thing most brutish," as Prospero says. On the other, some of his poetry suggests an intuitive sensitivity toward nature unlike that of anyone else in the play—he knows "every fertile inch o' th' island," and "all the qualities o' th' isle,/ The fresh springs, brine-pits, barren place and fertile." This sensitivity sets him apart from and above the civilized greed and vulgarity of Stephano and Trinculo. This contrast in Caliban is underlined in two of his speeches in this scene. In the first, at 91-94, he uses language which suggests the brutal Caliban—"brain him," "batter his skull," "paunch him with a stake," and "cut his wesand with thy knife." The verbs are all of savage physical destruction. This is the Caliban who would assault Miranda, and on whose nature "nurture will never stick." The second speech, at 140, is entirely different. It gives his reaction to Ariel's unearthly music, which terrifies Stephano and Trinculo, whom Caliban has to reassure with "Be not afeard." Shakespeare frequently defines his characters in terms of their reaction to music. As Lorenzo says in Merchant of Venice, "The man that hath no music in himself,/ Nor is not moved with concord a sweet sound,/ Is fit for treasons, stratagems and spoils . . . Let no such man be trusted." It is significant that where Stephano and Trinculo are frightened by the music, Caliban is moved to one of the most beautiful speeches in the play. The "sounds and sweet airs" induce in him a visionary, dreamlike state. He is able to perceive "riches" so wonderful that, waking, he cries to dream of them again. There is a surprising and moving pathos in the idea of Caliban, the "deboshed fish," being able to envision a world of lost beauty, a dream, barely remembered, of another, better world. The contrast with Stephano's complete lack of any kind of imaginative perception is made explicit in his rejoinder to this speech, in which he congratulates himself on the fact that, in his new kingdom, "I shall have my music for nothing."

But only Sycorax my dam and she;
But she as far surpasseth Sycorax
As great'st does least.
Stephano.   Is it so brave a lass?
Caliban. Ay, lord. She will become thy bed, I 107
   warrant,
And bring thee forth brave brood.
Stephano. Monster, I will kill this man: his daughter and I will be king and queen, save our Graces! and Trinculo and thyself shall be viceroys. Dost thou like the plot, Trinculo? 112
Trinculo. Excellent.
Stephano. Give me thy hand. I am sorry I beat thee; but while thou liv'st, keep a good tongue in thy head.
Caliban. Within this half hour will he be asleep. Wilt thou destroy him then?
Stephano.   Ay, on mine honor.
Ariel. This will I tell my master.
Caliban. Thou mak'st me merry; I am full of
   pleasure.
Let us be jocund. Will you troll the catch 121
You taught me but whilere? 122
Stephano. At thy request, monster, I will do reason, any reason. Come on, Trinculo, let us sing. 123
                      [*Sings.*
       Flout 'em and scout 'em 125
       And scout 'em and flout 'em!
       Thought is free.
Caliban. That's not the tune.

     [ARIEL *plays the tune on a tabor and pipe.* SD

Stephano. What is this same?
Trinculo. This is the tune of our catch, played by the picture of Nobody. 131
Stephano. If thou beest a man, show thyself in thy likeness. If thou beest a devil, take't as thou list. 133
Trinculo. O, forgive me my sins!
Stephano. He that dies pays all debts. I defy thee. Mercy upon us!
Caliban. Art thou afeard?
Stephano. No, monster, not I.
Caliban. Be not afeard: the isle is full of noises, Sounds and sweet airs that give delight and hurt not. 140
Sometimes a thousand twangling instruments
Will hum about mine ears; and sometimes voices
That, if I then had waked after long sleep,
Will make me sleep again; and then, in dreaming,
The clouds methought would open and show riches
Ready to drop upon me, that, when I waked,
I cried to dream again.
Stephano. This will prove a brave kingdom to me, where I shall have my music for nothing.
Caliban. When Prospero is destroyed.
Stephano. That shall be by and by: I remember the 151
story.
Trinculo. The sound is going away: let's follow it, and after do our work.
Stephano. Lead, monster; we'll follow. I would I could see this taborer: he lays it on. Wilt come?
Trinculo. I'll follow, Stephano.   [*Exeunt.*

107. "become": decorate suitably.

112. "plot": in the sense of both a) conspiracy, b) story.

121. "troll the catch": sing the song; a catch was a part-song for three or more voices, sung like our round.

122. "whilere": just now.

123. "reason": anything within reason.

125. "scout": make fools of.

SD. "tabor": small drum worn at the side.

131. "picture of Nobody": the reference is to the Elizabethan drawing of a man, Nobody, composed of head, arms and legs.

133. "as thou list": any way you like.

140. "airs": songs.

-happy when dreaming

151. "by and by": soon.

This scene returns us to the court party. The search for Ferdinand has led them through a frustrating maze of "forthrights and meanders" and Gonzalo and Alonso abandon the attempt to find him. Sebastian and Antonio are glad that Alonso sees the search as a hopeless one. They reaffirm their murderous intention.

At this point Prospero's magic intervenes. A banquet is presented to the wanderers which they are invited to eat. As soon as they approach, it vanishes. This is more than a complicated theatrical trick on Shakespeare's part. Traditionally, the offer of food represents the temptations of the world and the flesh. Eve was tempted by an apple; Christ by an illusory banquet. Here the banquet may be taken to represent not only sensuous enjoyment, but material (as opposed to spiritual) well-being. That is why the conspirators Sebastian and Antonio, who are committed to material values, are so ready to consume the banquet—"for we have stomachs." The disappearance of the food, and the denunciation by Ariel which follows, confirm the symbolic interpretation. The illusory quality of the repast indicates the illusory quality of the immoral, material values the "men of sin" pursue.

The presentation of this scene on the stage raises some interesting questions. It is often pointed out how little the Elizabethan theater could depend upon technical and mechanical devices. However, we do find occasional elaborate effects such as this one in Elizabethan plays. These were made possible because of a change in the first decade of the seventeenth century. The simple playhouses with bare stage and open roof (like The Globe) gave way to newer indoor playhouses, the precursor of our own theaters. Scenes involving lighting effects, or stage devices such as the vanishing banquet were possible in these indoor theaters. After 1608 Shakespeare's company used the indoor Blackfriars Theatre for many of its performances. The Tempest was almost certainly composed with the Blackfriars stage in mind. Mr. J. C. Adams has done much research into the staging of this scene in Blackfriars. He "conjectures, with plausible support from his knowledge of the powers and conventions of theatrical me-

Scene three.

(ANOTHER PART OF THE ISLAND)

Enter ALONSO, SEBASTIAN, ANTONIO, GONZALO, ADRIAN, FRANCISCO, ETC.

Gonzalo. By'r Lakin, I can go no further, sir: 1
My old bones ache: here's a maze trod indeed
Through forthrights and meanders. By your patience   3
I needs must rest me.

Alonso.   Old lord, I cannot blame thee,
Who am myself attached with weariness   5
To th' dulling of my spirits. Sit down and rest.
Even here I will put off my hope, and keep it
No longer for my flatterer: he is drowned
Whom thus we stray to find; and the sea mocks
Our frustrate search on land. Well, let him go.

Antonio. [*aside to* SEBASTIAN] I am right glad that
          he's so out of hope.
Do not for one repulse forgo the purpose   12
That you resolved t' effect.

Sebastian.   [*aside to* ANTONIO] The next
          advantage
Will we take throughly.

Antonio.   [*aside to* SEBASTIAN] Let it be tonight;   14
For, now they are oppressed with travel, they
Will not nor cannot use such vigilance
As when they are fresh.

Sebastian. [*aside to* ANTONIO] I say tonight. No more.
Solemn and strange music; and PROSPERO *on the top
(invisible). Enter several strange* Shapes, *bringing in a
banquet; and dance about it with gentle actions of saluta-
tions; and, inviting the* King ETC. *to eat, they depart.*
          SD

Alonso. What harmony is this? My good friends,
          hark!

Gonzalo. Marvelous sweet music!

Alonso. Give us kind keepers, heavens! What were
          these?   20

Sebastian. A living drollery. Now I will believe   21
That there are unicorns; that in Arabia   22
There is one tree, the phoenix' throne; one phoenix   23
At this hour reigning there.

Antonio.   I'll believe both;
And what does else want credit, come to me,   25
And I'll be sworn 'tis true. Travelers ne'er did lie,
Though fools at home condemn 'em.

Gonzalo.   If in Naples
I should report this now, would they believe me
If I should say I saw such islanders?
(For certes these are people of the island)   30
Who, though they are of monstrous shape, yet note,
Their manners are more gentle, kind, than of
Our human generation you shall find
Many — nay, almost any.

1. "By'r Lakin": by our Ladykin (a diminutive of the Virgin Mary).

3. "forthrights and meanders": straightforward and devious paths.

5. "attached": seized.

12. "for one repulse": because of one setback.

14. "throughly: thoroughly (a common Elizabethan form).

SD. "on the top": this may refer to a stage level above the upper stage, where the musicians sometimes sat. However if the banquet is brought on from the inner stage (as seems likely), Prospero may appear on the supper stage. He wears the "gown for to go invisible" (see I.ii.SD).

20. "keepers": guardian spirits.

21. "drollery": a puppet show.

22. "unicorn": this mythical beast is frequently referred to in Elizabethan drama.

23. "phoenix": another mythical Elizabethan favorite there was held to be only one phoenix at any time; the bird renewed itself from the flames of its own destruction.

25. "want credit": lack belief.

30. "certes": it is certain.

THE TEMPEST

ACT III SCENE III

chanics, that the table (with the banquet) which rises does so on a trap upon which, concealed by the hangings of the table, there lurks a stagehand. Ariel descends from the heavens on a 'machine' (probably a rope-and-pulley device); he covers the banquet on the table with his harpy's wings; whereupon the stagehand removes a panel in the table top and whisks the banquet (usually a light refreshment) out of sight. Ariel then lifts his wings, and by a 'quaint device' the banquet has indeed vanished" (Arden edition).

Ariel's speech at 53 makes clear the meaning of the vanishing banquet. The three "men of sin" in their own lives have desired the "banquet" of material wealth and power. On Prospero's island they must learn that such goals are illusory and deceptive. The three immediately draw their swords—they fall back on the ultimate worldly, material argument of violence. This is, of course, in vain. Ariel then forecasts a "ling'ring perdition" for them which they can only avert by the repentance of "hearts sorrow," and the subsequent innocence of "a clear life ensuing." It is sometimes said that, while Alonso does repent, Antonio and Sebastian do not, and yet they are spared at the play's end. But Ariel is here pronouncing their punishment ("worse than any death"), and Shakespeare's audience, conscious of the direct relation between sin and punishment, would view them as unrepentant, therefore, suffering sinners.

Prospero.   [*aside*] Honest lord,
Thou hast said well; for some of you there present
Are worse than devils.
Alonso.   I cannot too much muse
Such shapes, such gesture, and such sound, expressing
(Although they want the use of tongue) a kind
Of excellent dumb discourse.
Prospero.   [*aside*] Praise in departing.   39
Francisco. They vanished strangely.
Sebastian.   No matter, since
They have left their viands behind; for we have
    stomachs.
Will't please you taste of what is here?
Alonso.   Not I.
Gonzalo. Faith, sir, you need not fear. When we
    were boys,
Who would believe that there were mountaineers
Dewlapped like bulls, whose throats had hanging
    at 'em   45
Wallets of flesh? or that there were such men
Whose heads stood in their breasts? which now we
    find   47
Each putter-out of five for one will bring us   48
Good warrant of.
Alonso.   I will stand to, and feed;
Although my last, no matter, since I feel
The best is past. Brother, my lord the Duke,
Stand to, and do as we.

Thunder and lightning. Enter ARIEL, *like a harpy; claps
his wings upon the table; and with a quaint device the
banquet vanishes.*   SD

Ariel. You are three men of sin, whom destiny —   53
That hath to instrument this lower world
And what is in't — the never-surfeited sea
Hath caused to belch up you, and on this island,
Where man doth not inhabit, you 'mongst men
Being most unfit to live, I have made you mad;
And even with such-like valor men hang and drown   59
Their proper selves.

ALONSO, SEBASTIAN, ETC. *draw their swords.*

        You fools: I and my fellows
Are ministers of Fate. The elements,
Of whom your swords are tempered, may as well
Wound the loud winds, or with bemocked-at stabs
Kill the still-closing waters, as diminish   64
One dowle that's in my plume. My fellow ministers   65
Are like invulnerable. If you could hurt,   66
Your swords are now too massy for your strengths
And will not be uplifted. But remember
(For that's my business to you) that you three
From Milan did supplant good Prospero;
Exposed unto the sea, which hath requit it,   71
Him and his innocent child; for which foul deed
The powers, delaying, not forgetting, have
Incensed the seas and shores, yea, all the creatures,
Against your peace. Thee of thy son, Alonso,

39. "Praise in departing": from the proverb, "Do not praise the host's meal until you have eaten it."

45. "Dewlapped": a reference to the goitrous formation found in some European mountain dwellers.

47. "in their breasts": an Elizabethan travelers' tale, also referred to in *Othello*, ". . . men whose heads/ Do grow beneath their shoulders."

48. "Each putter-out . . . one": the Elizabethan voyager could deposit a sum in London which was forfeit if he failed to return, and repaid five-fold if he returned safely.

SD. "harpy": a mythical beast having the head of a woman and the body, wings and talons of an eagle; supposed to act as an agent of vengeance.
"quaint": ingenious, clever; the reference is to some sort of mechanical stage device.

53. "You": Alonso, Antonio and Sebastian.

59. "such-like valor": i.e., of madness.

64. "still": constantly.

65. "dowle": small feather.

66. "like": just as.

71. "requit it": avenged the usurpation.

THE TEMPEST

ACT III SCENE III

Alonso's beautiful speech at 95 indicates his state of mind. The whole of nature seems to "sing" his "trespass." His sin seems to him now an offense against the natural order of creation, not simply a political crime. He leaves the stage in despair, to "lie mudded" with the son he believes has been drowned as a punishment to him. He will, of course, be pardoned by Prospero. It is significant that Sebastian and Antonio, who sought to advance themselves by violence, are now "made mad." Their madness takes the form of insane, purposeless violence as they rush from the stage brandishing their swords against an enemy they can neither see nor understand. All the visitors to the island meet and undergo some sort of suffering, purgatorial experience. Ferdinand is made a log-carrying slave. The courtiers are driven mad. Stephano and Trinculo end in the depths of the horse pond.

Sebastian + Antonio wanted to eat the food and will be most severely punished — completely evil

Gonzalo, being innocent, has not heard the indictment and curse pronounced by Ariel. He therefore supposes that the three men's guilt has now begun to work upon them in the form of conscience, like a "poison." In his humanity, he sends the younger members of the party after them to try to save them from themselves.

They have bereft; and do pronounce by me
Ling'ring perdition (worse than any death   77
Can be at once) shall step by step attend
You and your ways; whose wraths to guard you from,
Which here, in this most desolate isle, else falls
Upon your heads, is nothing but heart's sorrow   81
And a clear life ensuing.   82

He vanishes in thunder; then, to soft music, enter the
Shapes *again, and dance with mock and mows, and*
carrying out the table.   SD

Prospero. Bravely the figure of this harpy hast thou
Performed, my Ariel; a grace it had devouring.   84
Of my instruction hast thou nothing bated   85
In what thou hadst to say. So, with good life
And observation strange, my meaner ministers   87
Their several kinds have done. My high charms work,   88
And these, mine enemies, are all knit up   89
In their distractions: they now are in my power;
And in these fits I leave them, while I visit
Young Ferdinand, whom they suppose is drowned,
And his and mine loved darling.   [*Exit above.*

Gonzalo. I' th' name of something holy, sir, why
     stand you   94
In this strange stare?

Alonso.   O, it is monstrous, monstrous!
Methought the billows spoke and told me of it;
The winds did sing it to me; and the thunder,
That deep and dreadful organ pipe, pronounced
The name of Prosper; it did bass my trespass.   99
Therefore my son i' th' ooze is bedded; and
I'll seek him deeper than e'er plummet sounded
And with him there lie mudded.   [*Exit.*
Sebastian.   But one fiend at a time,
I'll fight their legions o'er!
Antonio.   I'll be thy second.

     [*Exeunt* SEBASTIAN *and* ANTONIO.

Gonzalo. All three of them are desperate: their
     great guilt,   104
Like poison given to work a great time after,
Now gins to bite the spirits. I do beseech you,
That are of suppler joints, follow them swiftly
And hinder them from what this ecstasy   108
May now provoke them to.
Adrian.   Follow, I pray you.
     [*Exeunt omnes.*

sentencing

77. "perdition": punishment.

81. "is nothing but": i.e., the only way in which you can be protected. "heart's sorrow": repentance.

82. "clear": innocent.

SD. "mocks and mows": grimaces and gestures.

84. "devouring": i.e., making the banquet vanish.

85. "bated": omitted.

87. "observation strange": unusual attention.

88. "several kinds": various tasks.

89. "knit up": bound up; entwined.

94. "why stand you": Gonzalo has not heard Ariel's denunciation.

99. "bass my trespass": provide a bass, musically, for the statement of his guilt.

104. "their great guilt": Gonzalo assumes that their own knowledge of their guilt is now at work.

108. "ecstasy": madness.

THE TEMPEST

ACT IV SCENE I

Prospero's first speech explains Ferdinand's trial, which he has now successfully passed. The vexations he has undergone were trials of love, to establish his fitness to marry Miranda. Unlike the other members of the shipwrecked group, Ferdinand understands the nature of his trial. He accepts its difficulty since he understands that is a necessary preliminary to his fulfillment and happiness. Prospero then warns Ferdinand that Miranda's virginity must be preserved until the wedding. The length and vehemence of this warning has puzzled some commentators. Ferdinand, they maintain, has passed his test and established his fitness. Why does Shakespeare find it necessary to make Prospero appear a somewhat waspish, tyrannical father, unduly suspicious, and harping on an eventuality that he surely knows will not arise? Again the answer lies in one of the themes of the play: the difference between nature and nurture or, in this instance between the instincts of the natural man and the rules of civilized society. Caliban is present in the argument by implication. His attempted rape of Miranda was introduced by Shakespeare as part of the delineation of natural, instinctive behavior, uncontrolled by nurture, or the acquired laws of social living. Prospero knows the innocence of Ferdinand and Miranda. He also knows the "worser genius," natural appetite, that can "melt honor into lust." The elaborate warning about Miranda's chastity is not one father's apprehension in one particular case. It is a warning that social rule must always be present to quell the "fire i' the blood," or natural inclination. The marriage about to be celebrated is a ritual, ceremonial expression of the discipline that civilization should exercise over animal appetite.

(BEFORE PROSPERO'S CELL)

Enter PROSPERO, FERDINAND, *and* MIRANDA.

Prospero. If I have too austerely punished you,
Your compensation makes amends; for I
Have given you here a third of mine own life,   3
Or that for which I live; who once again
I tender to thy hand. All thy vexations
Were but my trials of thy love, and thou
Hast strangely stood the test. Here, afore heaven,   7
I ratify this my rich gift. O Ferdinand,
Do not smile at me that I boast her off,   9
For thou shalt find she will outstrip all praise
And make it halt behind her.
Ferdinand.   I do believe it   11
Against an oracle.
Prospero. Then, as my gift, and thine own acquisi-
    tion Worthily purchased, take my daughter. But
If thou dost break her virgin-knot before
All sanctimonious ceremonies may   16
With full and holy rite be minist'red,
No sweet aspersion shall the heavens let fall   18
To make this contract grow; but barren hate,
Sour-eyed disdain, and discord shall bestrew
The union of your bed with weeds so loathly
That you shall hate it both. Therefore take heed,
As Hymen's lamp shall light you.
Ferdinand.   As I hope   23
For quiet days, fair issue, and long life,
With such love as 'tis now, the murkiest den,
The most opportune place, the strong'st suggestion   26
Our worser genius can, shall never melt   27
Mine honor into lust, to take away
The edge of that day's celebration
When I shall think or Phoebus' steeds are foundered   30
Or Night kept chained below.
Prospero.   Fairly spoke.
Sit then and talk with her; she is thine own.
What, Ariel! my industrious servant, Ariel!

Enter ARIEL.

Ariel. What would my potent master? Here I am.
Prospero. Thou and thy meaner fellows your last
    service
Did worthily perform; and I must use you
In such another trick. Go bring the rabble,   37
O'er whom I give thee pow'r, here to this place.
Incite them to quick motion; for I must
Bestow upon the eyes of this young couple
Some vanity of mine art: it is my promise,   41
And they expect it from me.
Ariel.   Presently?   42
Prospero. Ay, with a twink.
Ariel. Before you can say "Come" and "Go,"
And breathe twice and cry, "So, so,"

Prospero-giving Miranda as a gift

3. "a third": this has been variously explained; Capell has suggested that Prospero's three thirds are Miranda, Milan and himself.

7. "strangely": remarkably; in a special way.

9. "boast her off": boast of her.

11. "halt": go slowly; limp.

16. "sanctimonious": sacred.

18. "aspersion": blessing.

23. "Hymen's lamp": Hymen, the Greek god of marriage, was usually represented as carrying a torch and a veil.

26. "opportune": the accent falls on the second syllable.

27. "worser genius": bad spirit. "can": i.e., can make.

30. "or Phoebus' . . . foundered": the sun-god's horses are lame; Ferdinand means that on that day he will not be able to wait for night to come.

37. "rabble": the rest of the spirits; not contemptuous in Elizabethan usage.

41. "vanity": display, show.

42. "Presently": at once.

THE TEMPEST

ACT IV SCENE I

Prospero now arranges a masque to celebrate the marriage of the two lovers. The masque was a special form of dramatic entertainment which had become popular at the court of King James in the first decade of the seventeenth century. It usually consisted of the dramatic representation of mythological personages (such as Iris and Ceres here) who acted out some simple situation to the accompaniment of dancing and music. Both the dancing and music might be elaborate, employing several groups or choruses, and a number of musicians. This was all performed before a background, or stage set, almost as complex as the settings for our own operas and musicals. The masque was thus a courtly and aristocratic, rather than popular, dramatic form. It was too elaborate for production on the stage of the simple, popular theaters, but was possible at Blackfriars. The masque in The Tempest would be particularly appropriate for a wedding, and the play was performed at court for the Elector Palatine, a German ruler who had come to marry James's daughter Princess Elizabeth.

Some commentators have pointed out that the language of the masque is more ornamental and artificial than is usual in Shakespeare's dramatic verse. They have suggested that it was written by a collaborator. To argue in this way is to say, in effect, that Shakespeare was incapable of altering his style to fit varying contexts. That we know to be untrue. The verse is formal and artificial because that was the sort of language required in a masque, as Shakespeare well knew. It must be remembered that the poetry of the masque is spoken to the accompaniment of dancing and music. For this reason it is somewhat simpler than Shakespeare's more dramatic verse. The audience cannot attend to complexity of movement, melody, and language simultaneously. When you compare the language of a poem that is to be read with one intended to be sung to music, you will find the language of the latter much simpler.

Each one, tripping on his toe,
Will be here with mop and mow.   47
Do you love me, master? No?
   Prospero. Dearly, my delicate Ariel. Do not approach
Till thou dost hear me call.
   Ariel.   Well: I conceive. [*Exit.* 50
   Prospero. Look thou be true: do not give dalliance 51
Too much the rein: the strongest oaths are straw
To th' fire i' th' blood. Be more abstemious,
Or else good night your vow!
   Ferdinand.   I warrant you, sir.
The white cold virgin snow upon my heart
Abates the ardor of my liver.
   Prospero.   Well. 56
Now come, my Ariel: bring a corollary 57
Rather than want a spirit. Appear, and pertly! 58
No tongue! All eyes! Be silent.   [*Soft music.*

Enter IRIS.   SD

Iris. Ceres, most bounteous lady, thy rich leas
Of wheat, rye, barley, fetches, oats, and pease; 61
Thy turfy mountains, where live nibbling sheep,
And flat meads thatched with stover, them to keep; 63
Thy banks with pioned and twilled brims, 64
Which spongy April at thy hest betrims 65
To make cold nymphs chaste crowns; and thy broom
    groves, 66
Whose shadow the dismissed bachelor loves,
Being lasslorn; thy pole-clipt vineyard; 68
And thy sea-marge, sterile and rocky-hard,
Where thou thyself dost air — the queen o' th' sky, 70
Whose wat'ry arch and messenger am I, 71
Bids thee leave these, and with her sovereign grace,
Here on this grass-plot, in this very place,
To come and sport: her peacocks fly amain. 74
Approach, rich Ceres, her to entertain.

Enter CERES.

Ceres. Hail, many-colored messenger, that ne'er
Dost disobey the wife of Jupiter,
Who, with thy saffron wings, upon my flow'rs
Diffusest honey drops, refreshing show'rs,
And with each end of thy blue bow dost crown
My bosky acres and my unshrubbed down, 81
Rich scarf to my proud earth — why hath thy queen
Summoned me hither to this short-grassed green?
Iris. A contract of true love to celebrate
And some donation freely to estate 85
On the blessed lovers.
   Ceres.   Tell me, heavenly bow,
If Venus or her son, as thou dost know,
Do now attend the queen? Since they did plot
The means that dusky Dis my daughter got, 89
Her and her blind boy's scandalled company 90
I have forsworn.
   Iris.   Of her society
Be not afraid: I met her Diety 92
Cutting the clouds towards Paphos, and her son 93

47. "mop and mow": gestures appropriate to spirits.

50. "conceive": understand.

51. "Look thou be true": addressed to the lovers; perhaps Prospero turns and finds them in an embrace.

56. "liver": supposed by the Elizabethans to be the seat of passion.
57. "corollary": surplus.
58. "pertly": swiftly.

SD. "Iris": the female messenger of the gods, and also the spirit of the rainbow.
61. "fetches": vetches.
63. "stover": winter food for cattle.
64. "pioned and twilled": dug under by the current and protected by branches woven together (Arden edition).
65. "spongy": damp. "hest": command.
66. "broom groves": thickets of gorse.
68. "lasslorn": i.e., having lost his lass. "pole-clipt": pruned.
70. "queen o' th' sky": Juno.
71. "wat'ry arch": rainbow.

74. "peacocks": the bird usually associated with Juno.

81. "bosky": wooded, the opposite of "unshrubbed" later in the line.

85. "estate": give, make "in the state" of a gift.

89. "dusky": dark, with reference to the underworld ruled by Dis. "my daughter got": Dis, or Pluto, abducted Proserpine, Ceres' daughter, to the underworld.
90. "blind boy": Cupid, usually pictured as blindfolded. "scandalled": scandalous, since Cupid was associated with desire.
92. "her Deity": her divine majesty.
93. "Paphos": in Cyprus, and associated with the worship of Venus.

The masque celebrates a marriage and the characters are chosen accordingly. The notion of fruitfulness (fertility), is present in the form of Ceres, goddess of earth and harvest (she is "most bounteous . . of wheat, rye, barley, fetches, oats and pease"). Juno, queen of heaven, sends Iris, her messenger, to Ceres, thus indicating the divine blessing of the union. Iris is the goddess of the rainbow, a traditional symbol of the peace that comes after discord. It is a sign the storm is over, and the sun is emerging once again. This is an important element in this marriage, which signifies the end of the "tempest" —the crisis with which the play began—and the beginning of a new happiness and serenity. Venus and Cupid are introduced at 87, and they also carry a symbolic meaning to the Elizabethan audience. Throughout the Renaissance the figure of Venus represented the object of sensuous or appetitive desire. Her son, Cupid, symbolized the effects of this desire on the lover. He is portrayed as shooting arrows from his bow (the pain the lover experiences,) and as being blind (the irrationality of sensuous love). This is why the pair, with their "wanton charm," are banished from the marriage of Ferdinand and Miranda, a union based on more than simple, sensuous desire. The masque ends with the Nymphs acting the part of the "sunburned sicklemen," or harvesters, reiterating the idea of fruition and fertility.

Dove-drawn with her. Here thought they to have done 94
Some wanton charm upon this man and maid,
Whose vows are, that no bed-right shall be paid
Till Hymen's torch be lighted; but in vain. 97
Mars's hot minion is returned again; 98
Her waspish-headed son has broke his arrows, 99
Swears he will shoot no more, but play with sparrows
And be a boy right out.

Enter JUNO.

Ceres. Highest queen of state, 101
Great Juno, comes; I know her by her gait.
Juno. How does my bounteous sister? Go with me
To bless this twain, that they may prosperous be
And honored in their issue.

They sing.

Juno. Honor, riches, marriage blessing,
Long continuance, and increasing,
Hourly joys be still upon you! 108
Juno sings her blessings on you.
Ceres. Earth's increase, foison plenty, 110
Barns and garners never empty,
Vines with clust'ring bunches growing,
Plants with goodly burden bowing;
Spring come to you at the farthest 114
In the very end of harvest.
Scarcity and want shall shun you,
Ceres' blessing so is on you.
Ferdinand. This is a most majestic vision, and
Harmonious charmingly. May I be bold 119
To think these spirits?
Prospero. Spirits, which by mine art
I have from their confines called to enact
My present fancies.
Ferdinand. Let me live here ever!
So rare a wond'red father and a wise 123
Makes this place Paradise.

[JUNO *and* CERES *whisper, and send* IRIS *on employment.*

Prospero. Sweet now, silence!
Juno and Ceres whisper seriously.
There's something else to do. Hush and be mute,
Or else our spell is marred.
Iris. You nymphs, call Naiades, of the windring brooks, 128
With your sedged crowns and ever-harmless looks,
Leave your crisp channels, and on this green land 130
Answer your summons; Juno does command.
Come, temperate nymphs, and help to celebrate
A contract of true love: be not too late.

Enter certain Nymphs.

You sunburned sicklemen, of August weary, 134
Come hither from the furrow and be merry.
Make holiday: your rye-straw hats put on,
And these fresh nymphs encounter every one
In country footing. 138

Enter certain Reapers, *properly habited. They join with the* Nymphs *in a graceful dance; towards the end wherof*

94. "Dove-drawn": Venus' chariot was usually represented as being drawn by doves.

97. "in vain": i.e., Venus and Cupid have come in vain.

98. "Mar's hot minion": Venus was frequently made the lover of Mars in Greek mythology.
"is returned again": has gone back.

99. "waspish": able to sting (with his arrows).

101. "right out": outright, completely.

108. "still": continually.

110. "foison": abundance.

114. "Spring come to you": "Almost certainly the expression of a conventional wish for a Golden Age of winterless years, in which spring and autumn are simultaneous, or consecutive" (Arden edition).

119. "charmingly": for the Elizabethans the word 'charm' usually carried a reference to magic, as it does here.

123. "wond'red": to be wondered at.

128. "windring": a combination of winding and wandering.

130. "crisp": covered with small waves.

134. "sicklemen": scythe-men.

138. "footing": dancing.

THE TEMPEST

ACT IV SCENE I

At the end of the masque the stage direction indicates that Prospero "starts suddenly and speaks." Both Ferdinand and Miranda comment on his anger. Some commentators have asked why, since Prospero can foresee and control every development of the play, he is here allowed to give way to this "distemper." The Arden editor has this comment: "Prospero . . . is in the grip of the temperate man. We may accept Warburton's suggestion that Prospero's anger at this point is quite adequately motivated by ingratitude; Caliban's ingratitude recalls that of Antonio—to the one he gave the use of reason, to the other ducal power. The conspiracy afoot reminds him of the past twelve years, which are now being rapidly re-enacted." To this it may be added that Shakespeare must keep dramatic interest and anticipation alive in the audience. This can hardly be done if we are continually reminded that Prospero will arrange for everything to turn out well in the end. His own suspicion and apprehension, though implausible, keep the audience aware of the coming developments of the plot.

PROSPERO *starts suddenly and speaks; after which, to a strange, hollow, and confused noise, they heavily vanish.* SD

Prospero. [*aside*] I had forgot that foul conspiracy
Of the beast Caliban and his confederates
Against my life: the minute of their plot 141
Is almost come. [*to the* Spirits] Well done! Avoid!
   No more! 142

Ferdinand. This is strange. Your father's in some
   passion
That works him strongly.
Miranda.   Never till this day 144
Saw I him touched with anger so distempered. 145
Prospero. You do look, my son, in a moved sort, 146
As if you were dismayed: be cheerful, sir.
Our revels now are ended. These our actors, 148
As I foretold you, were all spirits and
Are melted into air, into thin air;
And, like the baseless fabric of this vision,
The cloud-capped towers, the gorgeous palaces,
The solemn temples, the great globe itself,
Yea, all which it inherit, shall dissolve, 154
And, like this insubstantial pageant faded,
Leave not a rack behind. We are such stuff 156
As dreams are made on, and our little life 157
Is rounded with a sleep. Sir, I am vexed.
Bear with my weakness: my old brain is troubled.
Be not disturbed with my infirmity.
If you be pleased, retire into my cell
And there repose. A turn or two I'll walk
To still my beating mind.
Ferdinand, Miranda.   We wish your peace.

[*Exeunt.* FERDINAND *with* MIRANDA.

Enter ARIEL.

Prospero. Come with a thought! I thank thee,
   Ariel. Come.
Ariel. Thy thoughts I cleave to. What's thy
   pleasure?
Prospero.   Spirit,
We must prepare to meet with Caliban.
Ariel. Ay, my commander: when I presented Ceres, 167
I thought to have told thee of it, but I feared
Lest I might anger thee.
Prospero. Say again, where didst thou leave these
   varlets? 170
Ariel. I told you, sir, they were redhot with
   drinking:
So full of valor that they smote the air
For breathing in their faces, beat the ground
For kissing of their feet; yet always bending
Towards their project. Then I beat my tabor;
At which like unbacked colts they pricked their ears, 176
Advanced their eyelids, lifted up their noses 177
As they smelt music. So I charmed their ears 178
That calf-like they my lowing followed through
Toothed briers, sharp furzes, pricking goss, and
   thorns, 180

SD. "heavily": dejectedly, in sorrow.

141. "minute": the time appointed for.

142. "Avoid!": be gone.

144. "works": agitates.
145. "distempered": out of temper, harsh.
146. "moved sort": troubled state.

148. "revels": the term was usually used for pageants and dances; here it has a more general sense, indicating the whole entertainment that Prospero has produced.

154. "which it inherit": who could occupy or possess it.

156. "rack": wisp of cloud.
157. "on": of.

167. "presented": introduced in the masque, the director of a masque was sometimes called the "presenter".

170. "varlets": low, uncouth characters.

176. "unbacked": that had never been ridden; unbroken.
177. "Advanced": raised.
178. "charmed": again the sense is of a magic charm.

180. "goss": gorse.

Which ent'red their frail shins. At last I left them
I' th' filthy mantled pool beyond your cell, 182
There dancing up to th' chins, that the foul lake
O'erstunk their feet.
 Prospero.   This was well done, my bird.
Thy shape invisible retain thou still.
The trumpery in my house, go bring it hither 186
For stale to catch these thieves.
 Ariel.   I go, I go. [*Exeunt.* 187
Prospero. A devil, a born devil, on whose nature 188
Nurture can never stick: on whom my pains, 189
Humanely taken, all, all lost, quite lost!
And as with age his body uglier grows,
So his mind cankers. I will plague them all, 192
Even to roaring.

  Enter ARIEL, *loaden with glistering apparel, etc.*

  Come, hang them on this line.

PROSPERO *and* ARIEL *remain, invisible. Enter* CALIBAN,
STEPHANO, *and* TRINCULO, *all wet.*

Caliban. Pray you tread softly, that the blind mole
  may not
Hear a foot fall. We now are near his cell. 195
 Stephano. Monster, your fairy, which you say is a
harmless fairy, has done little better than played the
Jack with us. 198
 Trinculo. Monster, I do smell all horse-piss, at
which my nose is in great indignation.
 Stephano. So is mine. Do you hear, monster? If
I should take a displeasure against you, look you —
 Trinculo. Thou wert but a lost monster.
 Caliban. Good my lord, give me thy favor still.
Be patient, for the prize I'll bring thee to
Shall hoodwink this mischance. Therefore speak
  softly. 206
All's hushed as midnight yet.
 Trinculo. Ay, but to lose our bottles in the pool —
 Stephano. There is not only disgrace and dishonor
in that, monster, but an infinite loss.
 Trinculo. That's more to me than my wetting. Yet
this is your harmless fairy, monster.
 Stephano. I will fetch off my bottle, though I be
o'er ears for my labor. 214
 Caliban. Prithee, my king, be quiet. Seest thou
  here?
This is the mouth o' th' cell. No noise, and enter.
Do that good mischief which may make this island
Thine own for ever, and I, thy Caliban,
For aye thy foot-licker.
 Stephano. Give me thy hand. I do begin to have
bloody thoughts.
 Trinculo. O King Stephano! O peer! O worthy 222
  Stephano, look what a wardrobe here is for thee!
 Caliban. Let it alone, thou fool! It is but trash.
 Trinculo. O, ho, monster! we know what belongs
to a frippery. O King Stephano! 226
 Stephano. Put off that gown, Trinculo: by this
hand, I'll have that gown!

The court party were deluded by the appearance of a banquet. Stephano and Trinculo are to be similarly taken in by the "glistering apparel" that Ariel hangs in their way.

The conspirators against Prospero's rule are already in a bad way. They have lost the mainstay of their courage—the bottle of sack—in the horse pond which, as Stephano admits, is not only a "disgrace and a dishonor" but "an infinite loss" as well. Trinculo then discovers the "apparel." The plotters are once again diverted from their object. Shakespeare makes two minor but significant

---

182. "filthy mantled": covered with filth.

186. "trumpery": the glistering apparel of the stage direction below.

187. "stale": a stuffed bird used as a decoy; here, simply decoy.

188-9. "nature Nurture": here "nature" represents uncivilized, animal being, while nurture is education and civilization in the broadest sense.

192. "cankers": festers.

195. "Hear": the hearing of the mole was proverbial.

198. "the Jack": the knave; also in the sense of jack o' lantern or will o' the wisp, which misled travelers.

206. "hoodwink": cover up.

214. "o'er ears": i.e., underwater.

222. "O King Stephano!": Trinculo discovers the glistering apparel.

226. "frippery": old-clothes shop.

Like Lord of The Flies

points here. First, the conspirators fall out again, this time over the division of the illusory spoils. Caliban wants none of them. Trinculo and Stephano have a brief struggle over a gown which Stephano wants and, as king-to-be, gets. The second point lies in the division between Caliban and the two Neapolitans over the value of the clothes. Paradoxically it is Caliban, the unsophisticated natural man, who sees in some way that the "apparel" is "but trash." In this he is contrasted to the two representatives of civilization, who are immediately taken in by the glittering bait of the clothes. Their values pertain to the superficial, outer coverings. Civilization for them is not only not skin-deep, it is only clothing-deep. The scene ends with their pursuit from the stage by dogs, which is fitting. Their rebellion has not sufficient dignity to require human opposition.

very important

become more + more barbari(c) as the clothes come off.

much like William Golding

Trinculo. Thy Grace shall have it.

Caliban. The dropsy drown this fool! What do you mean
To dote thus on such luggage? Let 't alone,   231
And do the murder first. If he awake,
From toe to crown he'll fill our skins with pinches,
Make us strange stuff.

Stephano. Be you quiet, monster. Mistress line, is not this my jerkin? [*Takes it down.*] Now is the jerkin under the line. Now, jerkin, you are like to lose your hair and prove a bald jerkin.   238

Trinculo. Do, do! We steal by line and level, an't   239
like your Grace.

Stephano. I thank thee for that jest. Here's a garment for't. Wit shall not go unrewarded while I am king of this country. "Steal by line and level" is an excellent pass of pate. There's another garment for't.   244

Trinculo. Monster, come put some lime upon your   245
fingers, and away with the rest.

Caliban. I will have none on't. We shall lose our time
And all be turned to barnacles, or to apes   248
With foreheads villainous low.

Stephano. Monster, lay-to your fingers: help to   250
bear this away where my hogshead of wine is, or I'll turn you out of my kingdom. Go to, carry this.

Trinculo. And this.

Stephano. Ay, and this.

A noise of hunters heard. Enter divers Spirits *in shape of dogs and hounds, hunting them about,* PROSPERO *and* ARIEL *setting them on.*

Prospero. Hey, Mountain, hey!   255
Ariel. Silver! there it goes, Silver!   256
Prospero. Fury, Fury! There, Tyrant, there! Hark, hark!

[CALIBAN, STEPHANO, *and* TRINCULO *are driven out.*

Go, charge my goblins that they grind their joints
With dry convulsions, shorten up their sinews
With aged cramps, and more pinch-spotted make them   260
Than pard or cat o' mountain.

Ariel.   Hark, they roar!   261

Prospero. Let them be hunted soundly. At this hour
Lie at my mercy all mine enemies.
Shortly shall all my labors end, and thou
Shalt have the air at freedom. For a little,
Follow, and do me service.   [*Exeunt.*

---

231. "luggage": junk.

238. "lose your hair": An old sailor's joke; the jerkin is "under the line," i.e., has crossed the equator, or equinoctial line. It was a tradition to shave the heads of sailors crossing the line for the first time.

239. "line and level": i.e., according to a carpenter's rule and level, accurately or properly.

244. "pass of pate": effort of wit (pate for head).

245. "lime": birdlime, which was sticky.

248. "barnacles": geese.

250. "lay-to": use.

255-6. "Mountain . . . Silver": the names of the dogs.

260. "aged": as come with age.

261. "pard or cat o' mountain": leopard.

THE TEMPEST

ACT V SCENE I

In this, the final scene, Shakespeare—through Prospero—gathers together the various plots that have developed on the island. Alonso is restored to Ferdinand and Ferdinand to Alonso. The court party, Stephano and Trinculo, and the bewitched mariners are brought together. Ariel is freed. Prospero resumes his ducal garb and prepares to return to Milan.

At the scene's opening the court party are still imprisoned, "distracted." Ariel reports the grief of Gonzalo at the plight of his comrades. Ariel confesses that were he human, he would be moved by their condition. Prospero's reaction is important. We have seen him angered at the end of the masque in IV.i. He now confesses that he has been enraged at the memory of "their high wrongs" toward him. Now he is in a position to wreak his vengeance on them. Had this been one of Shakespeare's history plays, that is what he would have done. Here, however, he takes his cue from Ariel's pity, and relents. Shakespeare gives Prospero a line which sums up one of the meanings of the play: "The rarer action is/ In virtue than in vengeance." Here virtue is made to carry a good many meanings—humanity, charity, love, good faith—which are the opposites of an-eye-for-an-eye retribution. The idea of mercy expressed here recurs throughout Shakespeare's work. Portia gives expression to it in the great "quality of mercy" speech in Merchant of Venice. It is put even more directly in the sonnet lines: "They that have the power to hurt and will do none . . . They rightly do inherit heaven's graces." Prospero has been sort of a deity through the play, controlling the elements and directing the actions of the rest of the characters. He has rich cause for vengeance, but it is important to establish that he is not a vengeful deity. Recall that Prospero typifies good, "white" magic.

ACT FIVE, scene one.

(BEFORE PROSPERO'S CELL)

Enter PROSPERO *in his magic robes, and* ARIEL.

Prospero. Now does my project gather to a head.
My charms crack not, my spirits obey, and time   2
Goes upright with his carriage. How's the day?   3
    Ariel. On the sixth hour, at which time, my lord,
You said our work should cease.
    Prospero.   I did say so
When first I raised the tempest. Say, my spirit,
How fares the King and 's followers?
    Ariel.   Confined together
In the same fashion as you gave in charge,   8
Just as you left them — all prisoners, sir,
In the line grove which weather-fends your cell.   10
They cannot budge till your release. The King,
His brother, and yours abide all three distracted,
And the remainder mourning over them,
Brimful of sorrow and dismay; but chiefly
Him that you termed, sir, the good old Lord Gonzalo.
His tears run down his beard like winter's drops
From eaves of reeds. Your charm so strongly works
    'em,   17
That if you now beheld them, your affections   18
Would become tender.
    Prospero.   Dost thou think so, spirit?
    Ariel. Mine would, sir, were I human.
    Prospero.   And mine shall.
Hast thou, which art but air, a touch, a feeling
Of their afflictions, and shall not myself,
One of their kind, that relish all as sharply   23
Passion as they, be kindlier moved than thou art?   24
Though with their high wrongs I am struck to th'
    quick,
Yet with my nobler reason 'gainst my fury
Do I take part. The rarer action is   27
In virtue than in vengeance. They being penitent,
The sole drift of my purpose doth extend
Not a frown further. Go, release them, Ariel.
My charms I'll break, their senses I'll restore,
And they shall be themselves.
    Ariel.   I'll fetch them, sir.   [*Exit.*
    Prospero. Ye elves of hills, brooks, standing lakes,
    and groves,
And ye that on the sands with printless foot   34
Do chase the ebbing Neptune, and do fly him
When he comes back; you demi-puppets that
By moonshine do the green sour ringlets make,   37
Whereof the ewe not bites; and you whose pastime
Is to make midnight mushrumps, that rejoice   39
To hear the solemn curfew; by whose aid
(Weak masters though ye be) I have bedimmed
The noontide sun, called forth the mutinous winds,
And 'twixt the green sea and the azured vault
Set roaring war; to the dread rattling thunder

2-3. "time . . . carriage": time's burden is light, i.e., there is little time left.

8. "gave in charge": commanded, charged to be done.

10. "weather-fends": protects from the weather.

17. "eaves of reeds": i.e., a thatched roof.

18. "affections": feelings.

23. "relish": feel.

24. "kindlier": used frequently by Shakespeare in a double sense, 1) more sympathetic, 2) more in accordance with my kind, which is human.

27. "rarer": both less frequent, and nobler.

34. "printless": leaving no footprint (on the wet sand).

37. "green sour ringlets": fairy rings formed by toadstools.

39. "mushrumps": mushrooms.

61

THE TEMPEST

ACT V SCENE I

Prospero's speech beginning at 33 has often been taken as an example of Shakespeare's late style, in which some of his greatest dramatic poetry was written. Note that the general content of the speech was taken from one of Shakespeare's favorite source-books—Golding's 1567 translation of the Latin poet Ovid's Metamorphoses. Elizabethans had no scruples about borrowing generously from other writers, taking the sensible view that if they could improve on the original writer so much the better for them and the worse for him. Shakespeare often borrows in this way. A comparison of his source and what he makes of it does more than any amount of criticism to demonstrate his poetic method. Note the compressed, vivid power Shakespeare could give someone's routine writing. Here are the original lines from Golding:

Ye airs and winds: ye elves of hills, of books, of woods alone,

Of standing lakes, and of the night, approach ye everyone.

Through help of whom (the crooked banks much wondering at the thing)

I have compelled streams to run clean backward to their spring.

By charms I make the calm seas rough, and make the rough seas plain

And cover all the sky with clouds and chase them thence again.

By charms I raise and lay the winds, and burst the viper's jaw,

And from the bowels of the earth both stones and trees do draw

Whole woods and forests I remove: I make the mountains shake,

And even the earth itself to groan and fearfully to quake.

I call up dead men from their graves, and thee O lightsome moon

I darken oft, though beaten brass abate thy peril soon.

Our sorcery dims the morning fair, and darks the sun at noon.

Have I given fire and rifted Jove's stout oak 45
With his own bolt; the strong-based promontory 46
Have I made shake and by the spurs plucked up 47
The pine and cedar; graves at my command
Have waked their sleepers, oped, and let 'em forth
By my so potent art. But this rough magic
I here abjure; and when I have required
Some heavenly music (which even now I do)
To work mine end upon their senses that 53
This airy charm is for, I'll break my staff,
Bury it certain fathoms in the earth,
And deeper than did ever plummet sound
I'll drown my book.   [Solemn music.

Here enters ARIEL *before; then* ALONSO, *with a frantic gesture, attended by* GONZALO; SEBASTIAN *and* ANTONIO *in like manner, attended by* ADRIAN *and* FRANCISCO. *They all enter the circle which* PROSPERO *had made, and there stand charmed; which* PROSPERO *observing, speaks.*

A solemn air, and the best comforter 58
To an unsettled fancy, cure thy brains,
Now useless, boiled within thy skull! There stand,
For you are spell-stopped.
Holy Gonzalo, honorable man,
Mine eyes, ev'n sociable to the show of thine, 63
Fall fellowly drops. The charm dissolves apace; 64
And as the morning steals upon the night,
Melting the darkness, so their rising senses
Begin to chase the ignorant fumes that mantle 67
Their clearer reason. O good Gonzalo,
My true preserver, and a loyal sir
To him thou follow'st, I will pay thy graces 70
Home both in word and deed. Most cruelly 71
Didst thou, Alonso, use me and my daughter.
Thy brother was a furtherer in the act.
Thou art pinched for't now, Sebastian. Flesh and
        blood,
You, brother mine, that entertained ambition,
Expelled remorse and nature; who, with Sebastian 76
(Whose inward pinches therefore are most strong),
Would here have killed your king, I do forgive thee,
Unnatural though thou art. Their understanding
Begins to swell, and the approaching tide
Will shortly fill the reasonable shore, 81
That now lies foul and muddy. Not one of them
That yet looks on me or would know me. Ariel,
Fetch me the hat and rapier in my cell.
I will discase me, and myself present 85
As I was sometime Milan. Quickly, spirit! 86
Thou shalt ere long be free.

        [*Exit* ARIEL *and returns immediately.*

        Ariel sings and helps to attire him.

    Where the bee sucks, there suck I;
    In a cowslip's bell I lie;
    There I couch when owls do cry.
    On the bat's back I do fly
    After summer merrily.
Merrily, merrily shall I live now
Under the blossom that hangs on the bough.

45. "rifted": made a rift in, split.
46. "bolt": thunderbolt.
47. "spurs": roots.

53. "their senses that": the senses of those whom.

58. "air": the music.

63. "sociable to . . . thine": sympathetic to the sight of yours.
64. "Fall": let fall.

67. "mantle": cover, conceal.

70. "graces": virtues.
71. "Home": to the utmost.

76. "remorse": pity.
"nature": i.e.. the natural feeling for a brother.

81. "reasonable shore": the shore of reason, the mind.

85. "discase": take off the robe of invisibility.
86. "sometime Milan": i.e., when I was Duke of Milan.

THE TEMPEST

ACT V SCENE I

Shakespeare's first, most obvious improvement is in the rhythm of the verse. Golding's "fourteeners" (as the Elizabethans called the line, with reference to the number of syllables) are long, clumsy, trundling lines compared to the swift compression of Shakespeare's iambic pentameter. Shakespeare omits all that is clumsy in Golding ("I have compelled the streams to run clean backward to their spring".) He improves on everything he does use, as a point-by-point comparison of the two pieces will show.

The whole speech involves a question that frequently arises in discussions of The Tempest. Because the plays came at the end of Shakespeare's working life it is often suggested that in Prospero Shakespeare is portraying himself at the climax and completion of his career as a playwright. There is no external evidence to support this, but it is an attractive fancy. From this point of view the speech at IV.i.146 is directly relevant to the created world of Shakespeare's drama. His characters "As I foretold you, were all spirits," and the world of the plays is really no more than "the baseless fabric" of a "vision," which will dissolve like an "insubstantial pageant," leaving "not a wrack behind." In the speech in this scene, Shakespeare seems to be saying an even more direct farewell to his art. It is the "rough magic" which he will "here abjure." Having in his thirty-six-odd plays "worked his end upon the senses" of his audience with the "airy charm" of his art, he will at last "drown his book"—abandon the world of his plays and retire to Stratford—just as Prospero leaves his magic island for Milan. The Prospero-Shakespeare theory takes some strength from Prospero's epilogue. At the play's end, after his work as a magician performed before the audience, he throws himself on the audience's mercy. He asks for the reward of its applause. Whether or not there is anything in the notion that Prospero is Shakespeare, the applause has continued and increased for over four hundred years.

Prospero. Why, that's my dainty Ariel! I shall miss
    thee,
But yet thou shalt have freedom; so, so, so.
To the King's ship, invisible as thou art!
There shalt thou find the mariners asleep
Under the hatches. The master and the boatswain
Being awake, enforce them to this place,
And presently, I prithee.   101

Ariel. I drink the air before me, and return   102
Or ere your pulse twice beat.   [*Exit.*

Gonzalo. All torment, trouble, wonder, and amazement
Inhabits here. Some heavenly power guide us
Out of this fearful country!

Prospero.   Behold, sir King,
The wronged Duke of Milan, Prospero.
For more assurance that a living prince
Does now speak to thee, I embrace thy body,
And to thee and thy company I bid
A hearty welcome.

Alonso.   Whe'r thou be'st he or no,
Or some enchanted trifle to abuse me,   112
As late I have been, I not know. Thy pulse
Beats, as of flesh and blood; and, since I saw thee,
Th' affliction of my mind amends, with which,   115
I fear, a madness held me. This must crave
(An if this be at all) a most strange story.   117
Thy dukedom I resign and do entreat
Thou pardon me my wrongs. But how should
    Prospero
Be living and be here?

Prospero.   First, noble friend,
Let me embrace thine age, whose honor cannot
Be measured or confined.

Gonzalo.   Whether this be
Or be not, I'll not swear.

Prospero.   You do yet taste   123
Some subtleties o' th' isle, that will not let you   124
Believe things certain. Welcome, my friends all.
[*Aside to* SEBASTIAN *and* ANTONIO] But you, my
brace of lords, were I so minded,
I here could pluck his Highness' frown upon you,   127
And justify you traitors. At this time   128
I will tell no tales.

Sebastian.   [*aside*] The devil speaks in him.

Prospero.   No.
For you, most wicked sir, whom to call brother
Would even infect my mouth, I do forgive
The rankest fault — all of them; and require
My dukedom of thee, which perforce I know
Thou must restore.

Alonso.   If thou beest Prospero,
Give us particulars of thy preservation;
How thou hast met us here, who three hours since
Were wracked upon this shore; where I have lost
(How sharp the point of this remembrance is!)
My dear son Ferdinand.

Prospero.   I am woe for't, sir.   139

Alonso. Irreparable is the loss, and patience
Says it is past her cure.

[handwritten in margin: changing of Alonso]

101. "presently": immediately.
102. "drink the air": devour the space.

112. "enchanted trifle": magic trick.
    "abuse": deceive.

115. "amends": mends, improves.

117. "An if this be": if this is really so.

123. "yet": still.
124. "subtleties": (1) the usual meaning, (2) a special Elizabethan sense, meaning cooked confections representing mythical figures, common at banquets.

127. "pluck": pull down.
128. "justify": justly prove.

139. "woe for't": sorry for it.

63

THE TEMPEST

ACT V SCENE I

The court party are led in, still bewitched, "with frantic gesture." Prospero now puts aside his magic garment for the last time and appears "as I was sometime Milan," in preparation for the final denouement in which he confronts his enemies and reveals everything to them. Alonso who has already shown himself conscious of his sin, asks pardon "for his wrongs." Prospero embraces him, and Gonzalo, but in an aside to Sebastian and Antonio, indicates his knowledge of their treachery. At the play's end both Sebastian and Antonio would seem to remain unrepentant (but not necessarily unpunished: see commentary at II.iii), just as Stephano and Trinculo are not really changed by the ordeal they have undergone. We may think (as some have) that this gives the play an unfinished quality, until we reflect on how unconvincing and untrue to experience a neat ending, involving general forgiveness and general repentance, would have been. In our experience, as in Shakespeare's there are people who do not repent, who cannot evaluate and change themselves. Or like Stephano, they are constructed on such simple lines that they continue to behave in the same predictable way no matter what happens. In ending the play as he does Shakespeare is simply reflecting this truth.

Prospero.   I rather think
You have not sought her help, of whose soft grace
For the like loss I have her sovereign aid
And rest myself content.

Alonso.   You the like loss?

Prospero. As great to me as late; and, supportable 145
To make the dear loss, have I means much weaker 146
Than you may call to comfort you; for I
Have lost my daughter.

Alonso.   A daughter?
O heavens, that they were living both in Naples,
The King and Queen there! That they were, I wish
Myself were mudded in the oozy bed
Where my son lies. When did you lose your daughter?

Prospero. In this last tempest. I perceive these lords
At this encounter do so much admire 154
That they devour their reason, and scarce think
Their eyes do offices of truth, their words 156
Are natural breath. But, howsoev'r you have
Been justled from your senses, know for certain 158
That I am Prospero, and that very duke
Which was thrust forth of Milan, who most strangely
Upon this shore, where you were wracked, was
  landed
To be the lord on't. No more yet of this;
For 'tis a chronicle of day by day, 163
Not a relation for a breakfast, nor
Befitting this first meeting. Welcome, sir;
This cell's my court. Here have I few attendants,
And subjects none abroad. Pray you look in.
My dukedom since you have given me again,
I will requite you with as good a thing,
At least bring forth a wonder to content ye 170
As much as me my dukedom.

Here PROSPERO *discovers* FERDINAND *and* MIRANDA *playing
at chess.*   SD

Miranda. Sweet lord, you play me false.

Ferdinand.   No, my dearest love,
I would not for the world.

Miranda. Yes, for a score of kingdoms you should
  wrangle, 174
And I would call it fair play.

Alonso.   If this prove
A vision of the island, one dear son 176
Shall I twice lose.

Sebastian.   A most high miracle!

Ferdinand. Though the seas threaten, they are
  merciful.
I have cursed them without cause [*Kneels.*

Alonso.   Now all the blessings
Of a glad father compass thee about!
Arise, and say how thou cam'st here.

Miranda.   O, wonder!
How many goodly creatures are there here!
How beauteous mankind is! O brave new world
That has such people in't!

Prospero.   'Tis new to thee.

Alonso. What is this maid with whom thou wast
  at play?

145. "late": recent.

146. "dear": grievous.

154. "so much admire": are so amazed.

156. "do offices of truth": tell them the truth.

158. "justled from": jostled, or forced out of.

163. "chronicle of . . . day": something to be recounted over a period of days.

170. "a wonder": another play on Miranda's name.

S.D. "discovers": discloses, by pulling aside the curtain of the inner stage.

174. "Yes, for . . . play": i.e., Ferdinand may do what he likes to win, but Miranda will still consider it fair play.

176. "vision": another illusion.

THE TEMPEST

ACT V SCENE I

Prospero plays ironically with Alonso over the death of his son. He can sympathize, Prospero says, since he has himself lost a daughter "in this last tempest." The dialogue of the two fathers is a preliminary to opening the curtain of the inner stage (Prospero's cell) revealing the two children playing chess. Ferdinand's line "Though the seas threaten, they are merciful" sums up one aspect of the play's meaning that has special relevance for him and for his father. It is only through the tempest, and its consequent suffering, that they come to a fuller and richer life: love for Ferdinand, a new understanding for Alonso. Miranda's oft-quoted speech on viewing the newcomers has an ironic edge that she does not herself understand. To her immediate and innocent reaction "How beauteous mankind is . . . O brave new world" Prospero adds, in an aside directed to the audience, " 'Tis new to thee." She cannot comprehend the inhumanity of Sebastian, the ambitious cunning of Antonio, or even the wooden-headed egotism of Stephano. The only complete view of the world of Prospero's island is Prospero's. He is able to understand the evil of the court party, yet see the admiration of Miranda as, in its own place, proper and necessary. Gonzalo's speech at 205 again compresses much of the meaning of the play. It elaborates on Ferdinand's earlier line. It also recalls a progressive change in Shakespeare's drama from the earlier tragedies to the later romances. In the tragedies suffering did produce understanding. Hamlet, Lear and Othello all reach some sort of knowledge of themselves and the world. In each case the price of knowledge is the hero's suffering and death. In the romances the suffering is still present. While not as violent or dramatic as in the tragedies suffering is a necessary prelude to understanding, at least on the part of those characters who are capable of understanding. Those who suffered through the tempest and its aftermath "find themselves," in Gonzalo's phrase, "when no man was his own."

Your eld'st acquaintance cannot be three hours. 186
Is she the goddess that hath severed us
And brought us thus together?
   Ferdinand.   Sir, she is mortal;
But by immortal providence she's mine.
I chose her when I could not ask my father
For his advice, nor thought I had one. She
Is daughter to this famous Duke of Milan,
Of whom so often I have heard renown
But never saw before; of whom I have
Received a second life; and second father
This lady makes him to me.
   Alonso.   I am hers. 196
But, O, how oddly will it sound that I
Must ask my child forgiveness!
   Prospero.   There, sir, stop.
Let us not burden our remembrance with
A heaviness that's gone.
   Gonzalo.   I have inly wept,
Or should have spoke ere this. Look down, you gods,
And on this couple drop a blessed crown!
For it is you that have chalked forth the way 203
Which brought us hither.
   Alonso.   I say amen, Gonzalo.
   Gonzalo. Was Milan thrust from Milan that his
     issue 205
Should become kings of Naples? O, rejoice
Beyond a common joy, and set it down
With gold on lasting pillars: in one voyage
Did Claribel her husband find at Tunis
And Ferdinand her brother found a wife
Where he himself was lost; Prospero his dukedom
In a poor isle; and all of us ourselves
When no man was his own.
   Alonso.   [*to* FERDINAND *and* MIRANDA] Give me
     your hands. 213
Let grief and sorrow still embrace his heart 214
That doth not wish you joy.
   Gonzalo.   Be it so! Amen!

Enter ARIEL, *with the* MASTER *and* BOATSWAIN *amazedly*
                following.

O, look, sir; look, sir! Here is more of us!
I prophesied, if a gallows were on land,
This fellow could not drown. Now, blasphemy, 218
That swear'st grace o'erboard, not an oath on shore?
Hast thou no mouth by land? What is the news?
   Boatswain. The best news is that we have safely
     found
Our king and company; the next, our ship,
Which, but three glasses since, we gave out split, 223
Is tight and yare and bravely rigged as when 224
We first put out to sea.
   Ariel.   [*aside to* PROSPERO] Sir, all this service
Have I done since I went.
   Prospero.   [*aside to* ARIEL] My tricksy spirit! 226
   Alonso. These are not natural events; they
     strengthen 227
From strange to stranger. Say, how came you hither?

186. "eld'st": longest.

196. "I am hers": i.e., I am also her father (by marriage).

203. "chalked forth": indicated the direction.

205. "Milan . . . Milan": (1) the Duke, (2) the city.

213. "his own": i.e., master of himself.
214. "still": constantly.

218. "blasphemy": i.e., you blasphemous man.

223. "glasses": hour-glasses.
224. "yare": shipshape.

226. "tricksy": tricky, ingenious.

227. "strengthen": grow, increase.

THE TEMPEST

ACT V SCENE I

Perhaps the point that brings the action of the play to a close more aptly than anything else is the arrival of the ship's sailors, and Gonzalo's recognition of the Boatswain. We began the play with Gonzalo's fervent hope that the Boatswain would survive drowning to hang. Gonzalo himself recalls this when he sees the Boatswain again: "I prophesied, if gallows were on land/ This fellow could not drown." The sailors are followed by the members of Stephano's insurrection, among whom only Caliban is in any way changed by his experience—"I'll be wise hereafter,/ And seek for grace." Stephano and Trinculo are unrepentant and unregenerate, and indeed we would not have them otherwise. Who could imagine, or laugh at, or even sympathize with a Stephano who swore off sack and dedicated himself to moral rectitude?

Boatswain. If I did think, sir, I were well awake,
I'ld strive to tell you. We are dead of sleep
And (how we know not) all clapped under hatches;
Where, but even now, with strange and several
    noises
Of roaring, shrieking, howling, jingling chains,
And moe diversity of sounds, all horrible,   234
We were awaked; straightway at liberty;
Where we, in all her trim, freshly beheld   236
Our royal, good, and gallant ship, our master
Cap'ring to eye her. On a trice, so please you,   238
Even in a dream, were we divided from them
And were brought moping hither.

Ariel.   [*aside to* PROSPERO] Was't well done? 240

Prospero. [*aside to* ARIEL] Bravely, my diligence.
    Thou shalt be free.

Alonso. This is as strange a maze as e'er men trod,
And there is in this business more than nature
Was ever conduct of. Some oracle   244
Must rectify our knowledge.

Prospero.   Sir, my liege,
Do not infest your mind with beating on   246
The strangeness of this business: at picked leisure,
Which shall be shortly, single I'll resolve you   248
(Which to you shall seem probable) of every
These happened accidents; till when, be cheerful
And think of each thing well. [*aside to* ARIEL] Come
hither, spirit.
Set Caliban and his companions free.
Untie the spell. [*Exit* ARIEL.] How fares my gracious
    sir.
There are yet missing of your company
Some few odd lads that you remember not.

    Enter ARIEL, *driving in* CALIBAN, STEPHANO, *and*
      TRINCULO, *in their stolen apparel.*

Stephano. Every man shift for all the rest, and let 256
no man take care of himself; for all is but fortune.
Coragio bully-monster, coragio!

Trinculo. If these be true spies which I wear in my
head, here's a goodly sight.

Caliban. O Setebos, these be brave spirits indeed!
How fine my master is! I am afraid   262
He will chastise me.

Sebastian.   Ha, ha!
What things are these, my Lord Antonio?
Will money buy 'em?

Antonio.   Very like. One of them
Is a plain fish and no doubt marketable.

Prospero. Mark but the badges of these men, my
    lords,   267
Then say if they be true. This misshapen knave,   268
His mother was a witch, and one so strong
That could control the moon, make flows and ebbs,   270
And deal in her command without her power.   271
These three have robbed me, and this demi-devil
(For he's a bastard one) had plotted with them
To take my life. Two of these fellows you
Must know and own; this thing of darkness I
Acknowledge mine.

234. "moe": more.

236. "trim": sail.

238. "Cap'ring": dancing for joy.

240. "moping": not fully conscious.

244. "conduct of": the conductor of.

246. "infest": annoy.

248. "single": by myself, privately. "resolve": explain.

256. "Every man . . . himself": Stephano's confused version of 'All for one and one for all.'

262. "fine": i.e., finely dressed in his ducal costume.

267. "badges": signs worn by servants indicating whom they served.

268. "true": correct.

270. "flows and ebbs": i.e., of the tides.

271. "her": i.e., the moon's.

The action which began with a tempest ends, literally and symbolically, with the "calm seas, auspicious gales" promised by Prospero for the return to Milan.

Often in Elizabethan plays an "Epilogue" (usually played by a central character) follows the play to ask for the audience's applause. Prospero's speech may be viewed as (1) a traditional request for applause—"the help of your good hands" or (2) as evidence for the argument that the play is a personal allegory (see above). Here is one editor's paraphrase of it: "I am now outside the tale you have just followed just as I surrendered my powers in that tale, so I now stand before you stripped of imaginary glamour. One might say that the success of my enterprise as an actor is parallel to the happy outcome of my stage-plot."

Caliban.   I shall be pinched to death.

Alonso. Is not this Stephano, my drunken butler?

Sebastian. He is drunk now: where had he wine?

Alonso. And Trinculo is reeling ripe: where should they

Find this grand liquor that hath gilded 'em?   280

How cam'st thou in this pickle?

Trinculo. I have been in such a pickle, since I saw   282

you last, that I fear me will never out of my bones. I

shall not fear fly-blowing.   284

Sebastian. Why, how now, Stephano?

Stephano. O, touch me not! I am not Stephano, but

a cramp.

Prospero. You'ld be king o' the isle, sirrah?

Stephano. I should have been a sore one then.   289

Alonso. This is a strange thing as e'er I looked on.

Prospero. He is as disproportioned in his manners

As in his shape. Go, sirrah, to my cell;

Take with you your companions. As you look

To have my pardon, trim it handsomely.   294

Caliban. Ay, that I will; and I'll be wise hereafter,

And seek for grace. What a thrice-double ass   296

Was I to take this drunkard for a god

And worship this dull fool!

Prospero.   Go to! Away!

Alonso. Hence, and bestow your luggage where you found it.

Sebastian. Or stole it rather.

[*Exeunt* CALIBAN, STEPHANO, *and* TRINCULO.

Prospero. Sir, I invite your Highness and your train

To my poor cell, where you shall take your rest

For this one night; which, part of it, I'll waste   303

With such discourse as, I not doubt, shall make it

Go quickly away — the story of my life,

And the particular accidents gone by

Since I came to this isle; and in the morn

I'll bring you to your ship, and so to Naples,

Where I have hope to see the nuptial

Of these our dear-beloved solemnized;

And thence retire me to my Milan, where

Every third thought shall be my grave.

Alonso.   I long   312

To hear the story of your life, which must

Take the ear strangely.

Prospero.   I'll deliver all;   314

And promise you calm seas, auspicious gales,

And sail so expeditious that shall catch   316

Your royal fleet far off. — My Ariel, chick,

That is thy charge. Then to the elements

Be free, and fare thou well! — Please you draw

near.   [*Exeunt omnes.*

280. "gilded": flushed, made brighter in color than usual.

282. "pickle": in the senses of i) mess, predicament, ii) preservative (either the liquor he has drunk, or the horsepond).

284. "fly-blowing": i.e., since he is pickled, he will not decay as other meat does.

289. "sore": in pain.

294. "trim it": set it in order.

296. "grace": pardon, favor.

303. "waste": spend.

312. "Every third . . . grave": perhaps the other two thoughts will be for Miranda and Milan; or perhaps the meaning is simply that Prospero will give much thought to death.

314. "deliver": recount.

316. "sail": sailing.

THE TEMPEST

I behaved well in my fictitious character (and, I hope, acted well also); my fictitious reward is to return to Italy. To complete the parallel, you must release me from the bonds of failure as a performer. Just as Ariel in the fable speeds my ship, and brings my magical project to a successful conclusion, so must you, to ensure the prosperity of my theatrical venture, applaud me for the pleasure I have given you. I am now stripped of my stage powers, which might have enabled me to obtain this applause by daemonic agency; and I face the despair your disapproval would bring, unless this prayer to you succeeds; for I have still the power of every man to appear direct to the supreme mediating spirit, that of Christian mercy. I implore you to exercise mercy towards me, as you would have mercy procure forgiveness for your own trespasses" (Frank Kermode).

EPILOGUE

(SPOKEN BY PROSPERO)

Now my charms are all o'erthrown,
And what strength I have's mine own,
Which is most faint. Now 'tis true
I must be here confined by you   4
Or sent to Naples. Let me not,
Since I have my dukedom got
And pardoned the deceiver, dwell
In this bare island by your spell;   8
But release me from my bands   9
With the help of your good hands.
Gentle breath of yours my sails,
Must fill, or else my project fails,
Which was to please. Now I want   13
Spirits to enforce, art to enchant;
And my ending is despair
Unless I be relieved by prayer,
Which pierces so that it assaults
Mercy itself and frees all faults.
As you from crimes would pardoned be,
Let your indulgence set me free. [Exeunt.

4. "confined by you": Prospero hands his magical authority over to the audience.

8. "your spell": i.e., your silence, lack of applause.

9. "bands": bonds; Prospero means that he cannot leave the stage until they have applauded him with their "good hands."

13. "want": lack.

68

Caliban's plot to kill Prospero
Revenge or Justice?

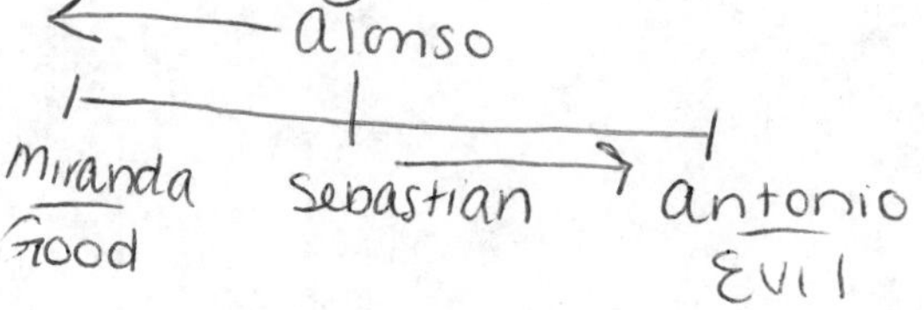

~~~~~~~~~~~~~~~~~~~~~~~~~~~~

Question Answers
5. Theme Of Repentence
   Gonzalo + Ferdinand - repent
major theme of play

Epiloague - Shakespeare asks
   for forgiveness through
   Prospero.

Forgives Antonio + Sebastian
   because he has been done
   wrong things, also.

King - becoming graces -
   - not only graces, but
     he wants those to acquire
     happiness.
Antonio + Sebastian -
   - deliberate cruelty
        - cruelty
   - absolute lack of repentence
   - "I must be cruel only to
        be kind"
        - not cruelty
Caliban - natural man
   - he knows that is very good
   - does know what is good

11. Change
   ⟵————— alonso
   |————————|————————→|
   Miranda Sebastian antonio
   Good   Evil

Discuss the Theme of education
· especially as it relates to Miranda
  + Caliban

Discuss the Christian Themes

Discuss the theme of chastity

Freudian analysis

Social hierarchy
· include imperialism, colonialism

Theme of Repentence.

Shakespeare's last play
· People say epilogue and 5th Act
  Last scene is Shakespeare's
  words to later people.

Certain Characters

goodness   Evilness
|_____
| characters throughout   10
            scale

microcosm -
Human Action - all happen in
Human Emotion   the setting
· Archetypes
· Stereotypes

cosm - 2 worlds

theme: knowledge and order

theme: Providence and patience
"There's a divinity that shapes
our ends rough now them how
we will."
"there's a providence in the fall
of a sparrow."

theme: Chastity and appetite

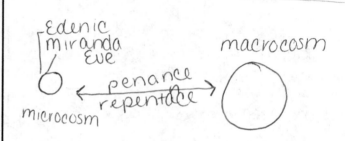

Pre-lapsarian   Post-lapsarian
     Pure Adam and Eve
  go back into macrocosm.
as king and Queen to
spread good in Earth.

NOTES

NOTES